Thinking about Christ
with Schleiermacher

THINKING ABOUT CHRIST WITH SCHLEIERMACHER

Catherine L. Kelsey

Westminster John Knox Press
LOUISVILLE • LONDON

Book design by Sharon Adams
Cover design by Lisa Buckley

First edition
Published by Westminster John Knox Press
Louisville, Kentucky

This book is printed on acid-free paper that meets the American National Standards Institute Z39.48 standard. ♾

PRINTED IN THE UNITED STATES OF AMERICA

03 04 05 06 07 08 09 10 11 12 — 10 9 8 7 6 5 4 3 2 1

Library of Congress Cataloging-in-Publication Data is on file at the Library of Congress, Washington, D.C.

ISBN 0-664-22594-2

Dedicated to the two men with whom I have been privileged
to learn to understand and appreciate Schleiermacher:
Richard R. Niebuhr, my mentor,
and
Terrence N. Tice, my love

Contents

Preface

This book invites you to take a reflective walk through one systematic approach to Christology, that of Friedrich Schleiermacher (1768–1834), in order to clarify the kinds of questions that Christology must address and how those questions interrelate. By virtue of beginning with an account of Christian experience of Christ, Schleiermacher assists faithful persons of many backgrounds to think theologically. His approach is especially helpful to Christians who want to find a way to think about their faith in a manner that is consistent with the best knowledge of their time and culture. The book is designed to use the richness and innovations in Schleiermacher's thought to launch you into your own systematic thinking about Christ.

Several features of this book are unusual. Throughout the chapters, you will find boxes that invite you to pause and relate the information you have just read to other experience and knowledge you have. Readers of Jane Vella's excellent work on teaching, *Taking Learning to Task: Creative Strategies for Teaching Adults*, will find some features here to be an adaptation of a strategy she has developed for adult learning.[1] The goal of this book on Christology is not simply to convey information about Schleiermacher's thought; instead, the book is designed to help the reader learn how to think with Schleiermacher about Christ—that is, interactively. Consequently this book assumes that the reader has some form of faith that is influenced by Christ, another unusual feature. The use of "we" throughout the book assumes that readers are exploring faith for themselves, which happens to be consistent with Schleiermacher's definition of theology as being for the church, the community of faith. So this book is meant to be a bridge between systematic language and thinking and

1

church language and faith. Bridges go both ways, and I hope readers gain confidence in moving back and forth between the two languages.

Don't let the style of this book fool you, however. This volume is a consistent interpretation of Schleiermacher's *Christian Faith* and the only thorough account of his Christology since Richard R. Niebuhr's.[2] Anyone wishing to grasp Schleiermacher's understanding of Christ must study *Christian Faith* and will find there a full account. For this reason, I have not attempted to refer to his *On Religion* nor have I made direct reference to his sermons. Although both are consistent with his account in *Christian Faith*, neither is necessary to grasp his Christology. Since this book is directed primarily to Christian insiders, Schleiermacher's account for insiders—in his mind, the community of faith within the churches—is most appropriate. That account is his *Christian Faith*.

One of the strengths of *Christian Faith* is its critical conversation with all of the significant alternative views at each point of doctrine. Another strength of *Christian Faith* is the consistency of its skeleton, built on the backbone of the experience of redemption. I have chosen to slight the former in order to make the latter very clear and to demonstrate its strengths and weaknesses as a skeleton. A variety of approaches to various points of Christology are acknowledged and explored in the boxes so that readers may think for themselves about alternatives to Schleiermacher's proposed account. The effort and time spent thinking about the questions posed in the boxes will be worthwhile. Scholars will recognize characterization of popular religious expressions and of most of the significant theological voices of the twentieth century appearing in those boxes, yet the reader will not be overwhelmed with the names and details.

Christian Faith is a daunting work, although once one has a sense of its approach and organization, one can appreciate its masterful consistency and stunning creation of a substantially new approach to Christology. I have been intentional about introducing the ideas it contains in a different order from Schleiermacher's presentation of propositions. He presents propositions in order to build an argument, piece by piece. I have presented the unfolding of an idea in its major concepts. This different order is intended to assist readers who need to see the forest before they can attend to or remember features of the individual trees. An overview of the organization of this unfolding idea is provided in the final section of the first chapter. Earlier in that chapter, one also finds a list of specific goals for what a reader can accomplish while reading and thinking with Schleiermacher.

All translations from *Christian Faith* in this book are mine. I have provided references only to English translations of other works by Schleiermacher in order to keep from overwhelming novice theologians. Proposition numbers make it easy for scholars to find the corresponding German from which I worked.

Finally, I want to acknowledge and thank three persons. Don McKim, my editor, has been encouraging and insightful in his questions from the very inception of the work. Richard R. Niebuhr's Schleiermacher seminar at Harvard Divinity School was the turning point in my appreciation of the complexity of Schleiermacher's thought and the simplicity of his goal to articulate the faith of Christians. As dissertation advisor and mentor, Dick was and is unparalleled. Terrence N. Tice has been the spouse one dreams of—in turn supportive, sympathetic, pushy, and a theological conversation partner par excellence. While we both know Schleiermacher's thought very well, Terry probably loves the details more than I, and perhaps for that reason he claims only I could have written this book. I love what theology can do to set us free from the ideas that stand in the way of deepening our relationship with God. Schleiermacher's theology can set many people free from ideas that strain their relationship with God. My hope is that this book finds its way into the hands of those people in particular.

1

Stepping Up to a Conceptual Picture of Christ

However the history of Christian theology is told, it always includes a few extraordinary and bold persons of faith and penetrating thought: Augustine of Hippo, Thomas Aquinas, John Calvin, and Martin Luther. Friedrich Schleiermacher (1768–1834) belongs in this list because his thought moved theology into the modern era at the beginning of the nineteenth century. In the face of intellectual challenges to using Scripture as an absolutely accurate historical record, and political challenges that made the authority of religious institutions less certain, Schleiermacher's theology demonstrated a coherent alternative approach. This approach significantly influenced every major theologian in the nineteenth and twentieth centuries. In fact, Schleiermacher offered the first thoroughgoing innovation in theological reflection upon Christ in a millennium!

Together in this book, we explore Schleiermacher's conceptual portrait of Christ and think alongside the theologian as well. In his time, Schleiermacher was writing for intellectually sophisticated readers steeped in the history of theology and philosophy. Nevertheless, any thoughtful person of faith can use the basic questions with which he worked to organize one's own reflective view of Christ. Most of us have a collage of stories and ideas about Christ that we have accumulated over the years, some of which don't fit together very well. Schleiermacher examines those various pieces, weeds some out, and organizes the rest into a "picture" or "portrait" of Christ to create one coherent, consistent whole. This picture is not of what Jesus looked like; his appearance doesn't matter to faith. Schleiermacher's portrait uses concepts to show how Christ is the focal point for our faith relationship with God.

HOW TO USE THIS BOOK

Why would anyone read a book about a theology with which they might well disagree? In order to figure out for themselves what they believe and why they believe it. The fastest way to identify one's own understanding of the faith one lives is to compare and contrast it to someone else's understanding. Of course, a balance must be struck in choosing which understanding to compare one's own thinking to; if the approach you choose does not share your unshakeable commitments in common, those big differences send you down a path of thought that will have little connection and consequently will illuminate your own path very little. If, on the other hand, the understanding being used for comparison is exactly like your own (hard to find, but possible), then the comparison does not push you to clarify the difficult places where the ideas don't fit together well or don't quite describe the faith you actually live.

The account of one's understanding of the faith one lives is called theology. In this book, we use the systematic theology of Friedrich Schleiermacher to think about our understanding of our faith in God through Jesus Christ. Schleiermacher's systematic theology is useful for several reasons. First, he begins with the faith experience of Christians and he keeps referring back to it. Every Christian experiences faith of some kind, so we can think about what we experience as we go. We don't have to be Bible scholars or philosophers to start where Schleiermacher starts. Second, he also shares a commonly held assumption of Christians that our faith depends on Christ, so he begins his thinking sorting through what we experience in relation to Christ. Third, he assumes that one cannot be a Christian without a faith community. That is, he is describing the faith of the church, not just the faith of scholars. Fourth, he takes seriously all of the doubts and skepticism of the times and finds a way to understand faith without being inconsistent with our understanding from science and history. Schleiermacher thinks through the difficulties until he can show how our faith is consistent with our intellectual lives.

This book has several audiences in mind. Readers who simply want to think through their own understanding of Christ need only read this text and think about the questions that appear regularly in boxes throughout the text. Those questions can help you make comparisons and contrasts with your own experience and thinking. If you write notes to yourself about your answers (and other thoughts), you will find those notes helpful as you draw together your own thinking while reading the concluding chapter.

Readers who especially want to understand Schleiermacher will find a copy of *Christian Faith*, his systematic theology, helpful. Throughout this book, proposition numbers are provided in parentheses in the text (e.g., §98.1). These items in the text refer to some of the sections of *Christian Faith* in which the particular ideas at hand are discussed. If you look at these references, you will see that our discussion here pays attention primarily to the basic ideas Schleiermacher proposes and leaves out his discussion of how his ideas relate to other specific theological points of view. Our intent is to make a dense argument more transparent so that we don't lose our way going through it. We are looking at the complex skeleton of the book and how its parts interconnect so that when you read *Christian Faith* for yourself, you can see how everything else hangs on and supports that skeleton. Don't ignore the questions in the boxes, however! They also help you identify what is distinctive in Schleiermacher's thought.

This book is not long, and it is meant to be relatively easy to follow. But the book is also meant to help you think. The more pauses you take to ponder the ideas and to ponder your own faith experience, the more fruitful your reading time will be. In those pauses, connections and illuminating insights may come.

As you read and think about this book, you can expect to accomplish the following:

- You will reject the notion that systematic theological thinking is only for scholars and is useless to most pastors and laypersons.
- You will recognize that you need not divorce faith from rigorous critical thought that accepts the results and methods of the sciences.
- You will practice active reading: questioning an author, expanding on and connecting ideas to experience, and evaluating theological concepts (including your own).
- You will practice articulating the relationships among your own theological concepts.
- You will be able to identify your own starting point or foundation for the way you think about your faith.
- You will explore the dynamics of Schleiermacher's systematic account of Christ and redemption.
- You will be able to articulate the reason for and the need for at least three different approaches to a systematic theological account of Christ and redemption.
- You will be invited to imagine the possibility that you could live in union with God through Christ.

Schleiermacher offers us a systematic theology, meaning that all of the various ideas are interconnected and consistent with one another. If we find ourselves reading along and saying, "Yes, but what about . . . ?" we have begun exploring interconnections. Because of all those connections, evaluating one idea apart from all the rest is difficult. As we proceed, then, we will find ourselves revising our sense of the value of what Schleiermacher has done as more and more of the ideas fit together. For those people who are familiar with church language, we will encounter some surprises along the way. We try to notice those surprises, because they encourage us to be sure that we understand why a point is different from what we anticipated. At the end, when we have in mind all the ideas with their relationships to each other, we'll be able to identify the strengths and the limitations of the account of Christian faith that Schleiermacher presents.

Finally, if we expect theology to have answers for us so that we will know everything about God and have no remaining questions, we are going to be disappointed. Our relationship with God is not unlike relationships with a spouse or very close friends. In those relationships we don't ever expect that we will completely understand the other, but we do our best to think about what we have seen and experienced with them in order to be a more responsive partner or friend. Much as we want to be able to anticipate all their ways or have them always do things our way, we can't. The same is true of God, only more so. Theology cannot provide answers for us if that is all we seek. Theology will never help us to get God to do what we want God to do more of the time, and theology will never substitute for faith, for being in relationship with God. Instead, theology helps us think more carefully about the God whom we love and who loves us. Trying to articulate clearly for ourselves what we understand is one way of expressing our love. No matter how much is muddled in your mind along the way, or how many questions are left at the end of reading this book, your thinking efforts may be an expression of your love of God in Christ. So be it!

AN EXPERIENTIAL METAPHOR
FOR GOD-CONSCIOUSNESS

Some people think using logic:

> If X is true, then Y and Z are also true, based on the following argument. . . . And if Z is true, then A follows based on these arguments. . . .

Other people think using metaphors:

> If X is a tree, then Y would be the branches in relation to X, which highlights something about both X and Y. And Z would be roots in relation to X. But a tree doesn't have anything like C's relation to X. Time to skip over to an additional metaphor! If X is a race car, then C is. . . .

Both ways of thinking are useful. Logic can make for explanations that are easy to follow. Metaphors can help us observe details that might otherwise escape our attention and can help us to attend to multifaceted relationships. Sometimes a metaphor helps us to grasp something intuitively until we can work out all the details.

In approaching the complex and highly organized theology of Friedrich Schleiermacher, a couple of metaphors can give us an intuitive grasp of what he explained. That intuitive grasp could keep us from becoming lost in the details. So before we approach Schleiermacher's theology directly, we are going to explore an experience that can be a metaphor for Christ's God-consciousness, which is the key to redemption and the whole of Schleiermacher's Christology.

The central metaphor is an experience that most preachers have had at least a few times, and that we wish we had every time we preached. We can't make it happen, but poor preparation or emotional distractions predictably prevent it from happening. We don't notice it at the moment, because we are too focused to pay attention to ourselves. In those grace-filled moments, our attention and all our best skill is directed toward the congregation in front of us and toward being open to what God is using us to show or say at that moment. After the fact, we realize that we said more than we knew to say. Somehow God did something better or bigger than our best effort, yet God worked through that effort. Rather than a "God-and-me" experience, the experience is one of "God-through-me-toward-others."

Maybe you're not a preacher. Writers share similar experiences, as do visual artists and performers. Many novelists have described the writing process and how their characters took the story in a different direction than planned, or even how a central character suddenly appeared in the middle of the story without warning. Potters talk about helping the clay become what it wants to be. Musicians speak of allowing the music to enter them before they sound the first note. In all these experiences, the preacher, the novelist, the potter, or the musician is open and attentive to something more, some additional influence that is more significant than what the individual knows or is within himself or herself.

Here's where the Christology comes in. The experiences we have just named are fleeting, special moments. Imagine what it would be like if every moment of one's life had that quality of attention and openness to something more: every moment connected to the source of creativity and inspiration, every moment connecting the divine to the real circumstances of that moment. When discussing Christ, Schleiermacher was thinking about a man whose life was an unbroken series of those moments. Christ's entire life was like those precious moments that we receive as fleeting gifts of grace.

Schleiermacher did not argue his systematic theology from this metaphor. He argued logically and in the order that had become the pattern for organizing

Christian theology. But we will understand Schleiermacher better if we keep this metaphor in mind. Schleiermacher was a famous and powerful preacher. He almost certainly had this experience. If in the course of reading this book, the discussion seems to be getting abstract, ask yourself, "How does this idea connect to or does it help explain the experience of cooperation with the divine?"

Pause a moment and do two things with the information that you have been given so far:
1. Think about your own life experience and identify some occasion when you looked back and recognized that you had been cooperating with something from beyond yourself—the divine, a muse, however you named it. Bring that experience fully to mind so that you can easily refer back to it.
2. Try thinking ahead of our description of Schleiermacher's theology. Using your own experience as the metaphor, what if every moment of your life was like that moment? How would you describe your relationship to God if every moment were like that one experience? What kinds of moments would be absent from your life if every moment were like that one experience? Finally, where does the metaphor *not* fit—that is, what kinds of moments are a part of being human but could not be transformed so that they would be like that experience?

PREACHING PRESUPPOSITIONS: THE FOCI AROUND WHICH SCHLEIERMACHER BUILT HIS DOGMATICS

As the preaching metaphor begins to illustrate, Schleiermacher's theology is very closely related to his leadership of a community of faith. Another way to see this close relationship is to examine his preaching. The presuppositions that undergirded his preaching are the foci for which his systematic theology provides an intellectual context. In other words, the systematic theology provides a way of thinking about Christ, God, ourselves, and the world in which these presuppositions make sense.

A careful reading of Schleiermacher's preaching shows that the experience of redemption lies at the center of his understanding of Christian faith. He consistently presupposed three things concerning redemption. These three things were present for more than forty years of his preaching, in all kinds of settings, and with different biblical texts providing the themes for the sermons. Schleiermacher knew these presuppositions to be true in the context of a community of faith at worship. They did not need to be proved; they were self-evident in the community of faith as a result of the shared experience of redemption.

The first presupposition is that everyone who comes into the sphere of Christ's influence is aware that he is the Redeemer. Redemption comes through Christ. Note, first of all, that the presupposition is stated in the present tense and not in the past tense. Persons are still coming into the sphere of Christ's influence today, just as they did two thousand years ago. Coming into that sphere of influence takes a little time; it doesn't just happen in passing.

Schleiermacher often referred to the story of the encounters with Christ narrated in John 1:35–51 as an example. In that story, Andrew and another future disciple spent half a day with Christ. In that time, Andrew came to see him as the Redeemer and so went to bring his brother Simon to meet him. Half a day was enough time to be in the sphere of Christ's influence during his lifetime.

The sphere of Christ's influence is now mediated by the community of faith. Part of the reason for writing theology is to provide an account of how that influence continues from one generation to the next. We state only briefly here what is shown fully as we proceed in chapters 4 and 5. The possibility of living a human life that completely connects all aspects of our physical life with a sense of the presence of God within our immediate awareness was evident to anyone who came within the sphere of Christ's influence during his lifetime. When persons are drawn into the experience of the one who perfectly lived out this possibility, they find themselves (1) aware that they cannot achieve this possibility on their own power and (2) aware that through grace they can experience it, which is redemption. After the death and ascension of Christ, the possibility was visible in the lives of those people who were redeemed. The way in which the redeemed are taken up into the mind of Christ makes the possibility of redemption visible to the next generation. The redeeming influence of Christ today thus does not occur primarily through the biblical text. The redeeming influence of Christ extends today through the visible power of redemption in the lives of the redeemed community of faith. We catch the faith from seeing it at work in people we know rather than by reading about it in a book.

This first presupposition arose both from Schleiermacher's careful study of Scripture and from his keen pastoral observation of how awareness of redemption is kindled in human lives and hearts. The second presupposition arose in the same way.

The second presupposition is that redemption is available through Christ prior to his death and resurrection. This presupposition is important because it influences not only our understanding of the significance of Christ's death and resurrection, but also the criteria we use for historical investigation of the life of Jesus.

If redemption was available through Christ prior to his death, then his death cannot be the decisive act or event that causes redemption. Schleiermacher read the faith responses of Jesus' disciples as attested in Scripture to show that Peter, John, Andrew, Nathanael, and others had experienced redemption in their relationship to Christ during his lifetime. Through his suffering and death, Christ's God-consciousness was unbroken, which demonstrates its perfection under all human circumstance. Christ's death thus has real meaning for faith, but his death is not itself the act that redeems. The presence and activity of perfect God-consciousness in a real historical human life redeems. So the redemption that was available to Peter and the others during Jesus' lifetime is exactly the same as the redemption available to us today.

Presupposing that redemption was the same during Christ's lifetime as it is today challenges one of the important criteria used in historical-critical research on the New Testament texts. The criterion assumes that the experiences of Christ's death and resurrection were decisive and faith-shaping for the church that formed after them, so anything in the biblical text that reflects the faith of the post-Easter church was probably read back onto the memory of Jesus' ministry during his lifetime. For this reason, those accounts cannot be considered authentic to the historical Jesus. Schleiermacher's presupposition that redemption is experienced in the same way both before and after the crucifixion suggests that this criterion makes a false distinction between the historical Jesus and the faith of the church. We explore this point in chapter 5.

The third presupposition undergirding Schleiermacher's preaching is that redemption is directly associated with incorporation into a community of Christians. Schleiermacher did not equate such a community of Christians with the institutional church. He had in mind smaller, less formal, and more intimate circles of support and encouragement existing within the institutional forms. Christ drew the first disciples together into such community as part of their ongoing relationship to him. Since that first generation, one cannot even recognize the possibility of redemption apart from communities of faith whose members make their experience of redemption visible in the present historical moment. Because redemption through Christ must be visible in a living person in order for it to be recognized as a real possibility, Schleiermacher could say that if every Christian were to die and a surviving non-Christian were to find and read the New Testament, that reader could not experience redemption. Schleiermacher's observation of Christian faith was that it is highly relational; we need each other in order to receive and nurture the faith.

This relational character runs through the entire systematic theology. Only in relationship to Christ are we redeemed. We perceive that possibility for relationship with God through Christ by seeing it active in the lives of persons with whom we are presently in relationship. Everything we know or believe about Christianity can be traced directly back to that experience of redemption through Christ (§11). We know what we know only as a result of relationship to Christ. As we shall see in chapter 3, examining the experience of redemption is where Schleiermacher began his theological thinking, and everything else follows from that starting place.

Pause a moment and compare your own understanding with Schleiermacher's. Noting the differences between your own presuppositions and his will allow you to distinguish where you disagree because he has not argued clearly and where you disagree because your experience of faith is different. What two or three presuppositions lie behind all the ways you think about Christ? (If you are finding this question difficult to answer, you are beginning to appreciate what makes theology a challenging thought process.)

CHRISTIAN FAITH: THREE KEY PROPOSITIONS THAT ORGANIZE THE ACCOUNT OF CHRIST

I know of nothing better to desire for my life than the uniting of the podium and the pulpit.[1]

Schleiermacher was early in his fifth and longest assignment as a preacher when he wrote this sentence in 1810. He was pastor and preacher at Trinity Church in Berlin. A new university was organizing at that time in Berlin, and Schleiermacher was actively involved in developing the theology school. As a full-time pastor he began simultaneously lecturing on theology, ethics, the Bible, psychology, hermeneutics, practical theology, and dialectics (how thinking is organized). He continued to preach at least once a week and to offer two lecture courses (about nine lectures a week) until his death almost twenty-five years later in 1834.

In 1821 and 1822, at the age of fifty-three, Schleiermacher published his first complete account of Christian faith. The work was titled *Christian Faith According to the Basic Propositions of the Evangelical Church Presented in Their Connection*.[2] When he spoke about the work to friends and colleagues, he called it his *"Glaubenslehre"* or "teaching of faith." As we discuss in chapter 2, he was explicitly not writing a philosophy of religion derived from universal principles. He was providing an intellectually rigorous and consistent description of one way of understanding Christian faith in the context of German Protestantism. Some need existed for such an account because two major strands of Protestantism, the Reformed and the Lutheran, had just been merged in Prussia to form the official national church. As we shall see, Schleiermacher's account was innovative and prompted quite a bit of criticism. So in 1830 he published a second edition with an entirely new text but the same organization and ideas.[3] Only this second edition has been translated into English.[4] References in this book are to propositions and subsections in the second edition.

Schleiermacher organized *Christian Faith* in logical form. The second edition is laid out in 172 propositions. Each proposition is then clarified and distinguished from other theological ways of explaining. The logical organization invites us to start reading on page one, and for those of us who are strictly logical readers, this method is a good way to proceed. For the rest of us, dipping in at the beginning and then skipping to the middle to get the lay of the land can be helpful. One actually can follow Schleiermacher's own line of thought in this manner. He seriously considered organizing the argument by beginning with what is now in the middle.[5] So we're going to proceed through Schleiermacher's argument in something close to his alternative order. We're bound to grasp his thought one way or the other!

The original title pages in both editions of *Christian Faith* include two quotes in Latin from Anselm of Canterbury. They both reinforce the connection between this work of systematic theology and living faith.

> Nor do I seek understanding in order that I may have faith, but I have faith in order that I may understand. *Proslogion*

> For those who do not have faith do not experience, and those who do not experience do not understand. *Dei Fide Trinitatis*

Faith experience comes first, and understanding follows. Christians have faith through relationship to Christ. In assimilation to him we experience redemption. Because Christ is central to our faith, exposition of what is true about Christ, his work, and redemption are organizing features of Schleiermacher's theology, which is to say that Christology is at the center of his theology.

If we dip into *Christian Faith* at just three points (§11, §88, and §100), we can trace the backbone that holds it all together.

> §11 Christianity is a monotheistic mode of faith the piety of which is teleologically oriented. It essentially distinguishes itself from other such faiths in that everything in it is related to the redemption accomplished through Jesus of Nazareth.

Three aspects of this proposition provide important guides to Schleiermacher's approach and how he will develop it. The first is his use of piety as part of the definition. Piety refers to the combination of thought and emotion as they issue in practices of faith. Schleiermacher is not defining Christianity by what theologians have thought and said about it. He defines Christianity by the experience of the faithful. He reflects upon and comes to a way of accounting for complex relationships between grace and individuals and the community of faith. This theology attempts to given an intelligible account of the heart and mind's relationship to God through Christ. Schleiermacher's theology is not primarily an account of what Christians think or believe about faith, but of how faith itself is kindled and in what form it flourishes.[6]

The second important aspect is Schleiermacher's assertion that everything in Christianity is connected in one way or another to redemption through

Christ. He could have left out "redemption" and simply said, "Everything is connected to Jesus of Nazareth," but he didn't. We are told from the first definition of Christianity that the experience of redemption is central to Christianity's self-understanding. In Schleiermacher's view, Christianity is not focused upon Jesus as a teacher or healer or prophet. Christianity is focused upon the historical man, Jesus of Nazareth, as he redeems us. Thus, throughout *Christian Faith*, the title for Jesus that Schleiermacher most frequently uses is "Redeemer," because that is who Christ is for us. The German word he uses, *Erlöser*, means a person who releases or sets something free.

This central role for redemption in Christianity leads Schleiermacher to begin his theological thinking with a very careful examination of what we experience as a result of redemption. Then he asks, what must be true of the Redeemer in order for him to accomplish that redemption in a historical context? If Schleiermacher had been writing in the late twentieth century rather than in the early nineteenth century, he would have shown us all that thinking in a "phenomenology" of redemption. But such an approach would not have been convincing in his own time, and so we can see that analysis only as it lies behind what he wrote. We bring the full background thinking to the foreground in chapter 3 because it makes Schleiermacher's thought more accessible to us today.

The third aspect of this proposition that guides us through Schleiermacher's thought is his claim that Christianity is a teleologically oriented form of piety. The word "teleological" means to be proceeding toward a final goal of perfection. Schleiermacher's use of the term here already begins to shape the understanding of redemption. We are forewarned that redemption involves a process of change. Schleiermacher shows us that redemption has a beginning in our lives, but that it will continue until we are like the Redeemer—sinless and perfect. (No, that is not going to happen anytime soon!) Redemption is a process moving toward a final goal, implying that redemption is primarily something that happens to us, rather than something that satisfies God.

In popular piety today, one commonly hears a definition of redemption that makes it sound like a transaction taking place outside the human sphere. Such a definition might be stated simplistically as follows: "Humans sinned and God's justice has been affronted. In love, God would forgive us outright, but divine justice would then be compromised, and because God is perfect such a compromise is not possible. So, in love God sent the Son to pay the price of all the sins of the world by dying on the cross. Divine justice is satisfied. Divine love is satisfied. We who believe are redeemed for all time. The debt is paid."

List all of the ways that Schleiermacher's account of redemption (as we've discussed it so far) is different from this popular account of redemption.

What advantages can you see to each of these accounts? What disadvantages?

From those key pieces of the account that we found in §11, let us jump now to the middle. Schleiermacher put all of his arguments about what the world is like and what we experience of God in the world and the nature of sin in the first half of *Christian Faith*. But we're particularly interested in what he says about Christ, so we're going to skip over those arguments for now. We'll come back to the definition of sin in chapter 4 because we'll want clarity on what we're redeemed *from*. Right now, though, we want to begin to see *how* we are redeemed.

> §88 In this collective life, which goes back to the effectiveness of Jesus, redemption is brought about by him by virtue of the communication of his sinless perfection.

The proposition makes clear that redemption occurs because Jesus shared with us something about himself: his sinless perfection. Redemption is not the result of a teaching from Jesus, nor is it a result of his death or resurrection. The Redeemer made visible the possibility that a human being could be sinless and perfect. When we see that possibility fulfilled in Christ, we come to know that by drawing close to him we ourselves can be brought into sinless perfection as a gift of grace. This process is redemption. Further, sinless perfection is blessedness.

Immediately after defining redemption in this way, Schleiermacher acknowledges that his approach is not the only understanding of redemption that is current in the Protestant Church. He argues that his account is the original one held in the early church, but he recognizes other accounts as valid, so long as they meet both of the following criteria:

1. Every approach to blessedness must be traced back to Christ.
2. A community is formed in which nothing is sought to account for redemption beyond the influence of Christ, and nothing is neglected that is part of his influence.

> Pause a moment to consider these two criteria. Do they include or imply every aspect of redemption that you can bring to mind?
>
> Would your own understanding of redemption meet these two criteria?
>
> On the basis of your answers, what are the strengths and the weaknesses of these two criteria defining an acceptable account of Christian redemption?

Two traditional distinctions about Christ, the work of Christ and the person of Christ, are brought together in §88. In Schleiermacher's account, the work of Christ, redemption, occurs as a result of his sharing his inner reality, his sinless perfection. The person and the work of Christ are one thing. All he had to do was to share with persons who he was in himself.

When we recognize the sinless perfection of Christ, two things happen. First, we are immediately aware of how different we are from him—that is, we see our own sin more clearly than we had before. Second, we are also aware that by drawing close to him, we are set free from that sin. More than forgiveness, this act is a gracious communication of the power by which the Redeemer does not enter into sin in the first place. How that communication could have such an effect is made clearer in §100.

§100 The Redeemer takes up the faithful into the power of his God-consciousness, and this is his redeeming activity.

Taken together, §88 and §100 suggest to us what makes possible Christ's sinless perfection: his God-consciousness. This term, "God-consciousness," is subtle, and the subtlety is important. The term does not mean thinking about God or consciousness of God, as if God is an object "out there" separate from us. Neither is a parallel term in Schleiermacher's meaning, "self-consciousness," consciousness of ourselves, thinking about ourselves, or observing ourselves. Self-consciousness is consciousness arising from the self and can be aware of anything at all. In the same way, Christ's God-consciousness is his awareness that arises from God; it is the presence of God in him.

Recall the metaphor of the preacher cooperating with the divine as well as your experience that evokes that metaphor. Awareness arising from God, or God-consciousness, makes those moments extraordinary, not thinking about God. Allowing our awareness to be directed by God and filled by God so that the awareness is no longer really "our" awareness makes those moments. Christ is open and aware in that way at every moment; that is his God-consciousness. Every sensory awareness, every thought, and consequently every action cooperates completely with the deep awareness that comes from the divine.

Of course, God-consciousness may sometimes direct awareness toward God, and in those moments one actually recognizes oneself as being in the presence of God. But God-consciousness is the source of Christ's awareness wherever it is directed.

Schleiermacher says that the sensory consciousness (awareness coming from the five senses) is taken up into Christ's God-consciousness. Sensory consciousness is not eliminated in the presence of God-consciousness; sensory consciousness is integrated into awareness arising from God and is placed in appropriate context. That "taken up" is the same word Schleiermacher uses to describe the relationship between the faithful and Christ himself is no accident. The relationship between the operation of the God-consciousness and sensory consciousness within Christ is parallel to the relationship between Christ himself and the faithful. Our consciousness is not eliminated by being taken up into the power of Christ's God-consciousness, but this consciousness is integrated into awareness arising from God and placed in appropriate context.

This concept leads to a startling claim. We are taken up into Christ's God-consciousness in redemption; therefore we are becoming like him. Now no thought appears anywhere that we are going to be anything other than human as a result of redemption. So to be fully human means to be like Christ. Human beings are meant to be all the time what we are in those fleeting moments. Redemption brings us to our truest, most human selves—in which we are perfectly open to awareness arising from God.

By now, we should be asking ourselves questions about the nature of God-consciousness: where does it reside in our psychological makeup, and how is it evident in our thinking and doing? As you might guess, Schleiermacher's answer is thorough and will take a little time to unpack. In chapter 4, we carefully read the introductory propositions of *Christian Faith* to understand his answer.

WITHIN THE LIMITS OF THE CHALCEDONIAN DEFINITION OF ORTHODOXY

Because his result is so different from the orthodox formulations that came before it, we must be sure to notice one more thing about Schleiermacher's effort in offering his account of Christ the Redeemer. Schleiermacher fully intended to offer an account of Christ that is faithful to the Definition adopted by the ecumenical council held in Chalcedon in 451 C.E. This definition sets the boundaries for orthodox accounts of Christ in virtually all of Christianity.

The Definition of the faith proper uses concepts from Greek philosophy that assume an understanding of what it means to be human (which is no surprise since the Definition was written in Greek). Much of the later theological thought about Christ has focused upon explaining how those terms appropriately apply to Christ. Schleiermacher did not focus directly on the debate over those terms. Rather than begin with them, he offered an account of being human in which the Chalcedonian Definition's basic claims could make sense. His account offers one way to understand how Christ is "perfect in deity and humanness," "without confusion," "without change," "without division," and "without separation" "one person" "in two natures." These claims compose the fundamental claims of the Definition.[7]

Now a fair questions to ask is: why bother with all this theological explanation? Why not just turn to Scripture and tell the story of Jesus as it is told there? The ecumenical council was called in the first place because so many different ways to interpret the biblical account of Jesus are possible. Setting a definition became necessary so that interpreters of the story would not misrepresent Christ. For that reason, the council at Chalcedon struggled to provide a clear and precise definition concerning what is true about Christ.

Once explaining the need for the Definition, why bother with explaining *how* it is true that Christ is fully human and fully divine, one person in two natures? Why not just take that Definition on faith and leave it at that?

That question has at least two answers, one of which is individual and the other dealing with the community of faith. Many individuals find it impossible to have faith in what seems absurd to them. Accepting divine mystery is not the problem, but rather that what is claimed about the human realm must be intelligible in light of our historical experience of human life. Schleiermacher is one of these individuals and so are most theologians. We seek to bring all of ourselves into our faith relationship, including our understanding. That we should be able to understand at least our human experience of Christ and of redemption seems reasonable to us. So our faith seeks understanding to satisfy our wondering minds.

The community of faith seeks understanding for a different reason. We quite easily can delude ourselves and shade the truth so that it does not demand so much from us. The careful explanation of how Christ is fully human and fully divine helps prevent us from sliding into any of the errors that Schleiermacher so aptly described. Language about the divine is almost always metaphorical because we are talking about something that is beyond our full grasp. Each error is based upon a metaphor taken too far. Every metaphor has limitations, places where it is not true. Theological thinking helps us recognize those limits. For this reason, theological thinking is essential to the church's faithfulness to God in Christ.

Pause for a moment and make two lists for yourself, a list of reasons for taking the Chalcedonean statements about Christ on faith alone, and a list of reasons to make the effort to explain how those statements are true of Christ. More good reasons exist for each list than those we have named so far.

What social or political circumstances might make one approach more appropriate than the other?

PREVIEW OF HOW WE'LL EXAMINE THE PORTRAIT OF THE REDEEMER IN DETAIL

We now have an overall picture of Schleiermacher's Christology. We have viewed this picture as if it were an impressionist painting; we have stepped back for an overall sense of what is portrayed. This perspective allows us to stay oriented as we examine the details in the next several chapters. We return to an overall picture again at the end in chapter 7, when we evaluate what Schleiermacher has done. At that point we also review the theological inquiry in which we have engaged for ourselves alongside Schleiermacher.

The next step in examining Schleiermacher's conceptual picture of Christ is to take a look at the frame around the picture. Schleiermacher is quite clear about what dogmatic theology is and what it is not. This determination is part of the frame. Schleiermacher's vocation as a pastor oriented both him and his understanding of theology toward the life of the church. So we'll begin with a quick review of the highlights of Schleiermacher's career. Then we'll turn to his *Brief Outline of Theology as a Field of Study*, in which he tells us the tasks of each kind of theology.[8] We'll also discover his way of dealing with the diversity of ideas and practices within Christianity, and we'll come around the fourth side of the frame by discussing the typical ways that Schleiermacher sets up an argument. These four points will help us as we turn to close examination of the picture of Christ itself.

One of the significant innovations in Schleiermacher's thinking about Christ is the point from which he began, which provides the theme of his conceptual portrait of Christ. In chapter 3, we explore why a new beginning point seemed necessary in the historical context wherein Schleiermacher found himself. Other options for beginning points were and are available, so we briefly compare Schleiermacher's to some of the other options. Then we bring into the foreground the account of redemption and Christian hope that lies behind *Christian Faith* and flesh out that account. This necessitates exploring a key explanatory concept, *Urbildlichkeit*. Then we prepare for the next chapters by thinking about what is implied in the account up to that point.

Chapter 4 returns us to §88 and §100 (among others) as we examine how Schleiermacher systematically describes in *Christian Faith* what is identified in an account of redemption and Christian hope. The definitions of four terms convey the core ideas. We explore these terms and then identify the key assumptions that Schleiermacher has made. Finally, we clarify the difference between proof, substantiation, and warrant for faith so that we do not misunderstand what Schleiermacher intends to offer in his systematic theology.

The most close-up view of the picture comes in chapter 5 as we again pick up the question "What must be true of Christ if he is able to redeem?" We look in detail at Schleiermacher's description of God-consciousness and how it relates to our psychological, intellectual, and spiritual development. Schleiermacher argues that this God-consciousness is not altered by Christ's suffering or death, so we consider his explanation of why Christ *did* suffer and die. The historical fact of Christ's life is an important feature of Schleiermacher's account, so we conclude this close-up view by examining how Schleiermacher handled historical Jesus research both in his dogmatics and in his lectures on the life of Jesus.

By this point we will have examined the picture frame, the picture theme (redemption), and the main figure (Christ), all in detail. Some other interesting features of the picture still remain; Schleiermacher included interpretations of each of the classic theological terms having to do with redemption. We examine these key terms and diagram their relationships to each other. Schleiermacher also provides an interpretation of six aspects of the Jesus story we will not have touched upon yet (virgin birth, baptism, miracles, resurrection, ascension, and return for judgment). Finally we attend to the conclusion of *Christian Faith* and his account of the Trinity. Not only does Christ have a role there, the Trinity is the carefully chosen summation of Schleiermacher's entire theological account.

Having addressed each of these features of the conceptual picture of Christ that Schleiermacher paints for us, we conclude by considering a series of evaluative questions. Is this account faithful to the Chalcedonian definition of the faith? Is it faithful to the historical and contemporary experience of the faithful? Is it reasoned out consistently, and does it make sense in our intellectual context? Does it facilitate ethical action in the midst of social and political affairs? Does it allow bridges to be built to other communities? Does an account of redemption recommend itself to additional communities of faith as a beginning point for theological reflection upon Christ? By the time we arrive at these answers, you will not only be equipped to read Schleiermacher's *Christian Faith* for yourself, you will also have successfully engaged in your own theological reflection upon Christ and will have developed clear points of agreement and disagreement with Schleiermacher. Congratulations in advance! Now, let's get started. . . .

2

The Picture Frame

Four Contexts for
Understanding Christian Faith

Four topics can help prevent our misunderstanding Schleiermacher's account of Christ. His life story prevents us from thinking that his *Christian Faith* is rooted in philosophy. Rather, the book is rooted in a deeply relational faith in God through Christ. His *Brief Outline of Theology as a Field of Study* prevents us from thinking that *Christian Faith* is apologetic—that is, meant to convince us of the truth of Christian faith. Rather, *Christian Faith* explains the coherence of contemporary Christian experience of redemption through Christ and connects that contemporary experience to the early experience of faith in Christ. Schleiermacher's acceptance of diversity within Christianity prevents us from thinking that all other ways of expressing Christian doctrine are invalid, while at the same time providing us with guidance for discerning what might be false orthodoxy. Finally, we examine some of the ways that Schleiermacher builds an argument so that we do not confuse his own position with those he opposes. These four topics function in the same way that a picture frame does. They keep our eyes and minds from wandering from the picture itself.

A LIFE ROOTED IN FAITH

Friedrich Daniel Ernst Schleiermacher was born November 21, 1768, in Breslau, the son of a Reformed chaplain in the Prussian military. His mother's father and brother were both Reformed pastors, and his uncle taught church history at the university in Halle for many years. Although his father, Gottlieb, was away from home in the field with the troops for long periods, he was deeply influential on his son's faith and development. In 1778, Gottlieb Schleiermacher encountered the Brethren community at Gnadenfrei and at age fifty-five found himself converted to a more emotion-centered relationship to Jesus that invigorated his life and his preaching. Five years later, when Friedrich was fourteen, the entire family visited Gnadenfrei and applied for admission for him and his older sister, Charlotte, and his younger brother, Carl, to attend Brethren school. During the time they spent among the Brethren community in Gnadenfrei, Friedrich experienced his own conversion to a relationally focused faith in Christ.

Later in 1783, still age fourteen, he entered the Brethren school and community at Niesky. When he said good-bye to his parents, he could not have known it would be the last time he would see either of them face-to-face. His mother died within the year. Friedrich maintained an active correspondence with his father on personal and intellectual and faith issues until his father's death eleven years later. At Niesky he lived and studied in the context of a carefully organized community of about six hundred persons, one hundred of whom were students from across Europe. The days were structured by worship four times a day with monthly Eucharist that involved two days of preparation including confession, a love feast, and footwashing. Much of the study occurred in the small groups of six to eight students who lived together and composed a faith support group. He studied Latin and Greek and developed his love for the classics. Although the religious life was highly structured, the education was known for its humanism. No exams were given, and although students were closely directed, they worked very independently. This love of independent study had begun in his early childhood and was maintained throughout his life.

At age sixteen, Schleiermacher was old enough to enter the Brethren seminary at Barby. The next year and a half was tough. The school at Barby trained all of the Brethren clergy for Germany, England, and America. The seminary had a high investment in maintaining orthodox Brethren theology, which focused upon personal relationship to Jesus, and had a very specific belief in the power of his blood to atone for sins. No questioning of Scripture or of specific orthodox tenets took place. Unfortunately, Schleiermacher arrived to study at Barby at the age when he had the most questions about particular tenets of Brethren faith. In the community, doubt was perceived as a willful sin. Schleiermacher was in a bind. He cherished the community and its worship, but could not find a way in himself to accept the theological description of the faith relationships he shared. He was not alone in his struggle, and one of his student colleagues was asked to leave the school in December 1786. In January 1787, Schleiermacher openly shared his doubts with his father, who tried first to guide his son back into Brethren formulas; when that approach was unsuccessful, Schleiermacher's father disowned him. But his father did give him permission to write to his mother's brother teaching at Halle to see if his uncle would guide him in study at the university. Fortunately, Stubenrauch welcomed his nephew. Consequently at Easter in 1787, Schleiermacher entered the university at Halle, where his father made just enough funds available for him to study for two years.

Schleiermacher attended lectures at Halle on all aspects of philosophy by the most famous member of the faculty and continued his own study, primarily of philosophy, although his agreement with his father had been to continue his theological studies. At the time, about eight hundred of the eleven hundred students at Halle were studying theology. He also worked hard on English and French so that he could gain a position as a tutor when he finished, because ministry did not seem to be intellectually viable to him at the time.

Nevertheless, Schleiermacher studied under his uncle's guidance for an additional year in preparation for the written and oral exams required to become a Reformed clergyperson. He completed the first series of exams in the spring of 1790 at the age of twenty-one. In October, he moved to Schlobitten in eastern Prussia where he became tutor for the Dohnas, a distinguished, wealthy, and influential Prussian aristocratic family. He taught the six children still at home, ranging in age from nine to twenty, and fell in love with their warm social and intellectual life. This domestic experience awakened an appreciation of the arts and of social discourse that Schleiermacher cultivated for the rest of his life. During his time in Schlobitten, he began his preaching career, preaching every other Sunday in the family chapel. He sent his sermons to his uncle and another mentor for comment and began to study the preaching of other well-known preachers in Germany and England. Published sermons were a popular form of literature in that culture, so plenty of sources were available for study even away from the city.

In May 1793, Schleiermacher returned to Berlin to prepare for the final ordination exams, which he passed the following March at age twenty-five. While in preparation he supported himself with teaching in a small school and then at an orphanage. His lifestyle was hand-to-mouth, just as it had been during his study at Halle. Once having passed the exams, however, things changed quickly. He was assigned as the associate pastor to the Reformed congregation in Landsberg, where he began in the fall. He knew the congregation because his uncle's brother-in-law Schuman served it. In fact, Schleiermacher had visited with them on his way from Schlobitten to Berlin. Schuman was in failing health, and Schleiermacher came to have considerable responsibility for the congregation. This experience was his first as a pastor as well as preacher, and he discovered it was his calling. The only positions he accepted for the rest of his career included regular preaching and care of souls.

Two years later, at age twenty-seven, he was assigned to the Charity Hospital in Berlin as the Reformed pastor. Alongside a Lutheran pastor, he was responsible for preaching and moral instruction both in the hospital and the poor house. During Schleiermacher's chaplaincy at Charity, a number of changes occurred. Charity absorbed the patients from the nearby mental hospital after it burned. Then an enlargement of the hospital building was completed. Finally, reforms in the medical practice were instituted because of charges from Schleiermacher's colleague that nursing, food, and cleanliness were inadequate and that administrators were denying medical procedures that physicians ordered. Hospital life was active for Schleiermacher, as were his pursuits as an intellectual. He was introduced into the salon of Henrietta Herz, a prominent occasion for conversation among intellectuals from many fields. Schleiermacher wrote several important works for these intellectual friends, most notably *On Religion: Speeches to Its Cultured Despisers* in 1799.[1]

Accounts of Schleiermacher's life commonly portray this period of his life as if he were really interested only in his intellectual and social pursuits and as if his work as chaplain was a sidelight. This misinterpretation of the situation is unfortunate. Although Schleiermacher did not publish any of his sermons from Charity Hospital, he explained that the audience at Charity had quite specific needs that made the sermons of less interest to the general reading public. His manuscripts from the period include a piece thinking through the condition and causes of poverty and the responsibility of the civil community in caring for the poor. The appointment to Charity itself was perhaps beneath the aspirations of a young man who wanted to rise in social rank, but his position does not mean that Schleiermacher was not fully engaged in the ministry. After all, he turned down at least one opportunity to move to an appointment as pastor in charge of the Reformed congregation in one of the smaller cities in Prussia in order to stay at Charity.

In 1802, Schleiermacher was required to leave Charity Hospital and became the court chaplain in Stolpe in eastern Prussia. The city of Stolpe and the city church were Lutheran, but a tiny community of about 50 Reformed families resided there, most of whom were public servants sent to Stolpe. This congregation had little cohesion both because of its size and the mobility of the civil servants who were its members. Stolpe was a far cry from the community of faith that Schleiermacher had come to cherish and that had become his model for the church as a result of his education among Brethren communities. Fortunately, after two years, an unexpected opportunity arose.

In August 1804, the king of Prussia initiated academic worship services at his flagship university, which was Halle. The decision was part of a pattern of creating social cohesion through efforts at moral improvement. Schleiermacher was named extraordinary professor and university preacher at Halle that fall. Some difficulties in the faculty delayed the beginning of actual worship services until August 1806. In the meantime, Schleiermacher began to lecture. After only two months of worship services, Napoleon's army invaded Halle and the university was closed. Schleiermacher remained in Halle for some months, hoping for a change in the situation. As a new government was instituted under the direction of the French, Schleiermacher returned to Berlin and Prussian rule early in 1807.

Schleiermacher's final and longest pastorate was his twenty-five years at the Trinity Church in Berlin. He received what was called a "vocation" to the church in 1808, a kind of trial year during which the widow of the former pastor was allowed to live in the manse but Schleiermacher served as pastor. In 1809, he was officially installed as the Reformed pastor of the church. He also married in 1809, bringing the young widow of a good friend and her two children to Berlin. They had three additional children together.

The king originally formed Trinity Church as a dual-faith congregation, with both a Lutheran pastor and a Reformed pastor. Separate liturgies and separate catechisms were used for these two descendants of the Reformation. The congregation offered two services every Sunday morning, one in the Reformed tradition and one in the Lutheran tradition. They traded week by week which tradition had the early service and which one the later. The congregation also offered a Saturday late-afternoon preparatory worship service and a Sunday afternoon service for servants and others who worked Sunday mornings.

During Schleiermacher's pastorate at Trinity Church, the king initiated the union of the Reformed and Lutheran traditions into one Prussian church. Schleiermacher participated vigorously in encouraging the union, even while he criticized some aspects of how the united church would make decisions about congregational matters. Trinity was the first congregation to ratify the union and actually unite in every aspect. Schleiermacher's experience of dual-tradition ministry at Charity Hospital had prepared him well for this situation.

Trinity Church had a total occupancy of 1,650 persons on the ground floor and in three choirs. Almost one-third of this number were standing places for low-income persons (everyone else paid for a pew seat). The congregation included a wide range of incomes and education levels. In this context, and as a result of his published sermons, Schleiermacher became known throughout Germany for his preaching. The church was regularly full for the main service. During his lifetime, in fact, Schleiermacher was better known as a preacher than as a theologian. He was quite clear that preaching was his first calling, sharing the faith in Christ visible in him. During the quarter-century that Schleiermacher preached to the city of Berlin, he watched military battles with the French fought at the city gate in his parish, he engaged in political struggles with the king, and his congregation provided aid as the city's population doubled while the industrial revolution began in Prussia. A full 10 percent of the population of the city lined the streets for his funeral procession. Twenty thousand people stood outside in February 1834 to honor the sixty-five-year-old man they knew primarily as a preacher of the faith.

A survey of Schleiermacher's life is important because as we struggle with his theology, we should not lose sight of the fact that theology was not merely an academic pursuit for him. Rather, as a young man, he had worked through doubts about the doctrines of faith in order to come to an understanding of his very real experience of Christ that was intelligible in light of the most rigorous thinking of his time. He brought together his philosophical training with his pastor's observation of human lives and provided an account of Christian faith for reflective Christians.

In the years immediately following Schleiermacher's appointment to Trinity Church, a new university was formed in Berlin. Halle, where Prussia's flagship university was located, had been seized by the French and attached to a more subservient political state. Prussia needed a university, and the king determined to found it in Berlin. Schleiermacher offered formative suggestions for the overall organization of the university and in particular for its theology faculty. His arrangement of the relationships between the various disciplines did not catch on widely, but his emphasis on the unity of theological disciplines centered in preparing church leadership has deeply influenced theological education in the United States as well as Germany. He was the first dean of the theology faculty and offered two lecture courses every term until his death. His interests were wide-ranging, as were his lecture topics. In addition to lecturing on some portion of the New Testament every term, he also regularly lectured on dogmatics, church history, practical theology, the life of Jesus, and the organization of theology. Over the course of his career, he also offered lectures on hermeneutics (the art of interpreting texts), psychology, pedagogy (the study of teaching and learning), aesthetics, ethics, dialectics (the philosophical study of how we think and know), and the state. His thinking in most of these areas was seminal and helped shape the modern investigation of these fields. On the side, he also translated the dialogues of Plato from Greek into German, a translation that remains in use two hundred years later. Philosophers, theologians, translators, and educators still read his works.

However Schleiermacher's wide-ranging interests, powers of observation, and intellectual creativity might impress us, we must not lose sight of the core of the man. He was first and last a person of deep and abiding faith in Christ. Everything else was simply an appreciation of the overflowing, gracious gen-

erosity of God—an appreciation that is only fully possible because of the kin-
dling of God-consciousness in us through redemption in Christ. In Schleiermacher's thought, all the various disciplines and lines of investigation are
interconnected. His concepts and his approach throughout his work are consistent because he experienced and understood the world to be consistent. For
this reason, he could not be satisfied with separating faith from all other
understanding. He sought, and found, a way to be intellectually consistent that
was true to the depth of Christian faith.

> Pause a moment and notice which features of Schleiermacher's story strike you as being
> especially important.
>   Given what you now know about the time period and his role as a pastor, what would
> you expect Schleiermacher would avoid doing in his theology?
>   What similarities do you see between Schleiermacher's political and social and eco-
> nomic world and your own? Did any aspects of his story sound familiar?
>   We have assumed in this section that the historical context in which a theology is formed
> is important, that it will influence the experience of faith and how that experience is inter-
> preted. Do you agree with this assumption, or do you expect theology to be articulated
> once and for all time? Or do you have yet a third assumption about the endurance or time-
> boundedness of theology?

WHAT DOGMATICS AND CHRISTOLOGY
ARE AND ARE NOT

With this strong connection to the church in mind, we should not be surprised
that Schleiermacher describes theology as a field with a very practical purpose.
Rather than being speculative, theology is "positive," by which he means that
theology starts with observing what is the case at this moment in history rather
than beginning with universal principles (as philosophy might). Further,
Christian theology is intended to provide the analysis necessary for church
leaders to lead. The same information might be gathered in historical study or
in sociology or psychology, but apart from the goal of furthering the life of the
Christian church the study is not theological. Considering this goal for Christian theology, that theology is the responsibility of the many kinds of church
leaders, lay and clergy, seems only reasonable. Consequently, Schleiermacher
expects that everyone engaged in the various specialties in theology is a part
of the Christian community. He also expects lay leaders in the church to
engage in theological reflections.

Schleiermacher thought very carefully about the organization and relationships between the various aspects of systematic reflection on Christianity.

Up to 1811, when the first edition of his *Brief Outline of Theology as a Field of Study*[2] appeared, the strong tendency in comprehensive accounts of the field was to list and define each of the disciplines as a separate enterprise. Schleiermacher's approach showed the relationships between and the dependence of each discipline upon the others.

His description begins in an unexpected place. We would expect to begin either with the study of New Testament texts (exegetical theology) or with the historical Jesus. Schleiermacher begins instead with philosophical theology. The reason demonstrates his understanding of what is really involved in exegetical theology. The responsibility of exegetical theology is to do two things: first, to determine as accurately as possible the original reading of each text—that is, before errors occurred in copying. Second, exegetical theology determines which texts are not properly a part of the canon. By "canon" he means those writings from primitive Christianity—the first generation—that contain the "normative presentation of Christianity."[3]

How will a person doing exegesis be able to identify what is normative? By comparing it to the essence of Christianity that philosophical theology identifies. In order for us to make judgments in our critical study of the New Testament texts, we use a conception of the core of Christianity as a standard. Exegetes typically assume that the core will be clear to them from the text itself. Schleiermacher is aware that the diversity of New Testament texts forces an exegete to use criteria for judgment that come from outside the text. He simply argues that the identification of these criteria ought to be a topic for critical thought and debate before we approach the biblical texts. That task belongs to philosophical theology. Of course, the determinations of philosophical theology concerning the essence of Christianity are not arbitrary; they are tested against and validated by the various aspects of historical theology, including exegetical theology. The process intentionally moves back and forth between exegetical work and articulating a presentation of Christian faith so that the two activities refine each other.

Schleiermacher clearly takes seriously the diversity within the New Testament texts. He argues that because only Christ is perfect, erroneous ideas about Christ and about the formation of early Christianity were inevitably included in the New Testament by its less than perfect authors. Schleiermacher also assumes that texts from that time period which were not included in the New Testament may still contain some canonical material that can contribute to a normative presentation of Christianity.

Thus we can see why the first major division of theological study is philosophical theology. It articulates the core of Christianity that distinguishes it as a mode of faith from other faiths and presents the form in which Christian community exists. One of the significant tasks of philosophical theology is to define concepts and what is essential to Christianity in light of all of its diverse forms in the various denominations. Given all that diversity, the task requires more than just describing what exists; determining the essence of Christianity requires seeing the whole that lies behind the diverse expressions and putting it into words.

We've already looked once at Schleiermacher's own succinct description of the core of Christianity. This description comes in the introduction to *Christian Faith*, in the section he calls "propositions borrowed from philosophical theology."

> §11 Christianity is a monotheistic mode of faith the piety of which is teleologically oriented. It essentially distinguishes itself from other such faiths in that everything in it is related to the redemption accomplished through Jesus of Nazareth.

This sentence defines Christianity in relation to other faiths and names what is distinctive about Christianity. Schleiermacher never wrote a full philosophical theology, so we don't have more than his brief description in *Christian Faith* of what the terms mean. We don't have his detailed argument. If he were to have made one, we would expect—based on his definition of philosophical theology—that he would argue by showing us how this description fits the historical evidence and the diversity of contemporary Christian practice.

As we noted in chapter 1, Schleiermacher was intentional about including redemption in his description of the essence or core of Christianity. In his view, Christianity is not focused upon Christ's teaching or miracles or death or resurrection alone. The core of Christianity is the way in which everything about Christ comes together to effect redemption. As we discuss later in this chapter, other descriptions of the core of Christianity were current in Schleiermacher's day and are current in our own day. Schleiermacher recognized that different descriptions have validity. In fact, he argued that every church leader must have thought through the issues and determined for himself or herself what constitutes the core of Christianity.

Pause a moment to try your hand at writing down the essence or core of Christianity as you recognize it in your faith community. Try for just one sentence. You might look back at Schleiermacher's §11 for ideas on how to organize your sentence.

Here are some other options to start you thinking:

- Everything in Christianity is related to the emergence and completion of the reign of God proclaimed by Jesus.
- Everything in Christianity is related to the revelation found in the New Testament.
- Everything in Christianity is related to the ongoing work of the Spirit in the church.

- Everything in Christianity is related to the moral teaching of Jesus of Nazareth.
- Everything in Christianity is related to the atoning death of Jesus of Nazareth.
- Everything in Christianity is related to the resurrection of Jesus and the shattering of sin and death.
- Everything in Christianity is related to preparing for heaven.

Philosophical theology takes two additional steps that follow from its central purpose: (1) defending Christianity from attacks from the outside, which is called "apologetics," and (2) identifying diseased conditions within Christian communities, which is called "polemics." Under apologetics lies the task not only of responding to attacks but also of answering questions that are obvious to someone inside the faith. For instance, why is the Redeemer Jesus and not some other figure such as Gandhi or Buddha or Mohammed? Apologetics answers that kind of question.

Schleiermacher's *Christian Faith* is a systematic work of dogmatic theology; the book presents neither exegetical nor philosophical theology. What does dogmatic theology do? First, consider the two other branches of theology: historical theology and practical theology. Practical theology has to do with the actual tasks of the church. Historical theology is the link between philosophical theology and practical theology. Historical theology critically tests the claims made through philosophical theology. Such testing serves to show which claims Christian experience through the centuries can verify. Historical theology provides the foundation for acting in the future in light of the past and present condition of Christianity. Dogmatics is one aspect of historical theology.

Human beings are historical, which is another way of saying that we always exist in a context that has a past that led into the present and that impinges on future possibilities. To make decisions for the future, church leadership must have knowledge of the whole community to be led, both its present situation and how the community is a product of the past. Since Christianity is teleological, it is always in a process of change. Historical theology helps leaders avoid problems from the past (repeating them would be a regression) and thereby facilitates decisions that participate in God's fulfillment of creation.

Historical theology, then, has three parts: exegetical theology, which has to do with Christian origins (as we noted earlier); knowledge of the entire sweep of Christianity and its history, which is church history and history of dogma and morals;[4] and knowledge of the state of Christianity at the present time, which is church statistics and dogmatic theology.

Not simply a numerical counting of participants in the life of faith, church statistics includes all of the forms of reflection upon the different experiences of different communities and cultures as they influence the experience of Christian faith. Church statistics is the topic within which Schleiermacher took account of all the different perspectives and emphases within contemporary Christianity. He might have placed womanist and feminist and mujerista and black and Central American liberation theologies within this part of theology, had they emerged in his lifetime. He did place what became sociology of Christianity here. Church statistics is the part of theology that attends to the nitty-gritty variety of the present life of Christian community, the lived side of the present. Schleiermacher's emphasis on piety, the practices of the faith, as the point of departure for understanding Christianity makes the field of church statistics in his broad meaning of the term the more important aspect of historical theology as it describes the present, which is a sharp contrast to the traditional emphasis placed on doctrine.

We finally arrive at the place of doctrine in Schleiermacher's vision. Doctrine is what the church says it believes is involved in Christian faith. Different branches of Christianity thus have somewhat different doctrine. Dogmatic theology is a comprehensive description of Christian doctrine and morals that now has currency. Christian morals is included with the comprehensive description of Christian doctrine, because our understanding of faith has direct implications for how we treat each other and live in the world. These implications are articulated in Christian morals, and they change depending upon one's doctrine. Schleiermacher argues against our current tendency to separate ethics into a field that begins with principles derived in philosophy. He also argues against an unprincipled Christian morality that simply lists the "rules" for Christians. Instead, he argues for a reflective field that derives its principles as implications of faith in Christ, as that faith is articulated in particular doctrinal perspectives.

Pause a moment to examine a diagram of the relationships between these various areas of thought, which is the easiest way for many of us to grasp them. What surprises you? What is missing?

Philosophical theology	Historical theology	Practical theology
Apologetics	Exegetical theology	Church service
Polemics	Church history	Church governance
	History of the churches	
	History of doctrines	
	History of morals	
	State of the churches at present	
	Church statistics	
	Dogmatics and morals	

Dogmatic theology is clearly a sizable enterprise even though it is not the only task of theology. Dogmatic theology includes both doctrine and morals, as well as a description of every form of doctrine and morals that now has currency, not just our own doctrine. Can such a description be done in a single text? Probably not. Schleiermacher has defined the entire field, not what particular texts can do. Each text contributes to a larger task.

Having said that, we appear to have incorrectly assigned Schleiermacher's *Christian Faith* when we called it "dogmatic theology." Schleiermacher has not attempted to describe each of the various contemporary (for him) doctrinal expressions of Christian piety. In fact, he has not even attempted to describe each of the doctrinal expressions of piety that had currency within his own denomination, the Prussian Evangelical Church. Instead, he has offered a systematic description of one doctrinal understanding of Christian faith, not only as a description of what exists within the community of faith, but also as an invitation to this way of understanding the piety we share. His invitation is to a systematic reflection that is consistent with both piety and critical historical thinking. Schleiermacher argued that ecclesial interest and scientific interest cannot be allowed to contradict one another, but they must be worked with together until they agree.[5]

Why should ordinary church leaders bother with dogmatics? Why not leave it to the specialists? Dogmatics serves church leadership by giving "practical activity the norm for popular communication, this so as to guard against the recurrence of old difficulties and confusions and to prevent the introduction of new ones."[6] The clarity provided by a systematic presentation of doctrine makes it possible to decide that some ways of expressing faith are misleading, whether used in the context of worship or in teaching about the community's faith. Clear statements of the various presentations of doctrine that are current within the church allow affirmation of our common understandings and common experience in faith. Clear doctrinal statements also allow us to avoid branding each other falsely as misguided or heretical, thus creating unnecessary discord.

The exposition of a system of doctrine or systematic theology will make use of philosophical disciplines, which is to say, the very best means of thinking and arguing clearly and persuasively. In Schleiermacher's view, any philosophical system may be used to organize a system of doctrine, provided that the philosophical system does not exclude or deny the religious element of life in general nor what Christianity professes in particular. Thus, any philosophy that denies teleology would be excluded from use, as would atheist, materialist, or sensualist systems.[7]

Each doctrinal position taken in a systematic theology must be verifiable in two ways. A doctrine must refer its contents directly or indirectly to the New

Testament canon itself or to the ecumenical creeds. Notice the use of the "canon" rather than the whole of the New Testament. A specialist in dogmatic theology must be cognizant of the results of exegetical theology. Schleiermacher's description is of a highly interactive set of enterprises, testing themselves against each other in order to achieve the highest degree of consistency. In addition to verification by the canon, a doctrinal position must show its consistency with kindred propositions. Thus, a system of doctrine must be logically consistent within itself.

Now we've said a great deal about dogmatics and never mentioned Christology. How does it fit into the scheme? Christology is literally the study of Christ. Schleiermacher assigned historical study of the life of Jesus to history (not even a theological discipline) and to exegetical theology (when its purpose is to facilitate the work of the church). The life of Jesus is important—he lectured on Jesus' life several times—but it is not to be confused with Christology. Christology attends to one set of themes within dogmatic theology. If we agree with Schleiermacher's statement of the core of Christianity, then Christology attends to the most central themes of dogmatic theology, articulating the understanding of Christ that results from the experience of redemption through Christ. Schleiermacher is not saying that the experience of Christ conflicts with a historical account of Jesus' life, but the starting point is different. The starting point for the life of Jesus is all the historical texts and other material that inform our understanding of the first century. The starting point for Christology is reflection upon the particularities of Christian self-consciousness. The beginning of Christology is also a historical starting point, because Christian self-consciousness is a phenomenon in human history that has a historical cause, but the study of Christology has a different starting point than a study of the life of Jesus. Christology investigates what can be said to be true about Christ as a result of the faith that he elicits. Then Christology thematizes the doctrinal propositions, verifying them through reference to the canon and the ecumenical creeds and through testing of their logical consistency with one another. Just as dogmatic theology does not address the question "Why Jesus?" neither does its subfield of Christology. That question is left to apologetics. Christology begins its doctrinal account assuming a living faith in Christ. Christology, as a part of dogmatics, explains the inner coherence of the faith rather than convincing us of its truth. Conviction of the truth of faith comes to us as a gift of grace in encounter with Christ.

All of what we have described so far, philosophical theology (including apologetics and polemics) and historical theology (including exegetical theology, church history, history of doctrine and morals, church statistics, dogmatics, and Christian morals) is aimed to support the "crown of theology," practical theology. This is consistent with what Schleiermacher says about the purpose of theology as a whole: to provide what church leaders, lay and clergy, need in order to lead. The purpose of this leadership is not understood as the task of securing institutional maintenance and survival, but rather the care or guidance of souls. This understanding does not preclude church government as a necessary topic for practical theology, because the care of souls requires a community of faith in Schleiermacher's view. So the two main topics for practical theology are church government and church service.

Are we overwhelmed yet by what Schleiermacher shows us is our task as reflective church leaders? He is aware that the task is large and complex, but he is convinced that individual pastors can adequately absorb and integrate the elements necessary for the task and develop the skills for assessing the work of specialists upon which we must rely much of the time. After all, he was able to do all of this reflective work as part of his own pastoral practice! On the other hand, for twenty-five years he also taught persons preparing for ordained ministries and he could see the struggles that others had along the way. In fact, he discusses in *Brief Outline* the need to understand better how to introduce critical thinking about the faith to students. He had seen how the faith that students brought with them to seminary was at least initially weakened by learning to think critically about it.[8] He was not prepared to give up critical thinking, by any means! But he was concerned to support faith as new skills are being learned. This man really cared for souls.

So we come to the end of a long section defining one side of the picture frame and we have learned that Schleiermacher aptly chose the title for *Christian Faith*; the book is not a dogmatic theology because it only describes one systematic exposition of Christian doctrine. *Christian Faith* is, most accurately, a "teaching of faith," a *Glaubenslehre*. Further, we have learned that dogmatic theology is not the crown of theology, nor even its most determinative component. The crown is practical theology and the determinative component is philosophical theology because it names the core or essence of Christianity. Finally, we have seen that dogmatic theology and its subfield, Christology, are meant to explain the inner coherence of the faith to those people who already know its reality. The rest of the picture frame is going to be much easier to put in place now that we have two sides.

THE DIVERSITY WITHIN CHRISTIANITY

In Schleiermacher's view, has he provided the only valid systematic theology for Christians in his time or ours? No, he has not. But this conclusion does not mean that every systematic theology is a valid expression of Christian faith, nor that every valid systematic theology is equally valuable. Having said this,

Schleiermacher's acceptance and even anticipation of the diversity within Christianity is striking. His understanding of human beings as historical creatures who are influenced by our past and the present conditions in which we find ourselves translates into each aspect of the theological enterprise.

In philosophical theology, we saw that Schleiermacher insists that each church leader must determine for herself or himself how to articulate the core of Christianity. He was not anticipating that we would each come to the same wording or even the same "core," as can be seen in his telling us that different exegetical theologies and different dogmatic theologies and different accounts of church history will develop on the basis of different core understandings. He had in mind, in particular, that the difference would not disappear between the Roman Catholic Church and the Protestant Church (viewed as one reforming tradition). This contrast between Roman Catholic and Protestant was still during his lifetime a major theme within Christianity in Germany, three hundred years after Luther and Calvin. He believed that the core understanding of Christianity in the Roman Catholic Church was significantly different from the core understanding in the Protestant Church, even if the articulation of the two understandings might sound very similar. He did not address the differences with Orthodox Christianity or other branches of Christianity such as Armenian or Coptic, but the same expectation applies. If the core expression, the philosophical theology, is different, then Schleiermacher expected that the systematic doctrinal expression will also be different between different denominations within Christianity.

But what about within one denomination? Shouldn't we expect only one valid dogmatic treatment of doctrine within a denomination? Schleiermacher again says no. While one can only accurately write doctrine for the branch of faith that one practices, it is not "necessary that all treatments which relate to the same period of the same Church community should agree among themselves."[9] Schleiermacher thinks that Christianity is teleological—that is, changing and moving toward complete fulfillment in the indeterminate future. That position implies change, not only change in Christian moral practice (such as improving the consistency of our acting in accordance with our faith) but also change in understanding and doctrinal expression. How does he see such change occurring?

Schleiermacher sees theology advancing through an active balancing of two kinds of elements found in theology. The "orthodox" doctrinal element is that which holds fast to what is already generally acknowledged within Christianity as doctrinally valid.[10] These orthodox elements are essential because they maintain unity. But if they are the only elements used in theology, no change and therefore no possible growth in theological understanding will occur. A false orthodoxy strictly holds to propositions that are "entirely antiquated" and that no longer directly influence other propositions in the doctrinal system.[11] The "inclination to keep the conception of doctrine mobile and to make room for still other modes of apprehension" is the "heterodox" doctrinal element. These elements make room for different apprehensions of the core of Christianity as it is seen in a period, all of which may lay claim to being ecclesial. They also make room for a new dominant core of Christianity to emerge. On the other hand, a false heterodoxy challenges well-grounded doctrinal propositions that are integrated into a critically reasoned system of doctrine that is accepted within the church. The balance between orthodox and heterodox elements makes progress in theology possible and the imbalance of the same elements makes regress in theological understanding occur.

The opponents that Schleiermacher primarily had in view as he wrote both *Brief Outline* and *Christian Faith* could easily be seen to side exclusively with one or the other of these elements. But that assessment is not exactly accurate, so we'll investigate them just a little further. Schleiermacher positioned himself in contrast to what he called super-naturalists on the one hand and rationalists on the other (they would probably not have chosen these labels for themselves). Schleiermacher's objection to the super-naturalist descriptions of Christ is that they make Christ so divine that seeing how he could be a real human being, even if a perfect one, is virtually impossible. If Christ was not fully human, then he was not the completion of human nature, and thus not able to be the promise of the fulfillment of creation (called the "second Adam" by the apostle Paul). Schleiermacher's concern to avoid super-naturalism is consistent with the early christological formula that what Christ did not embody he did not redeem. This formula requires us to find a way to understand Christ as fully human, although unique.

The rationalists, on the other hand, are problematic because they reduce what Christ does to redeem us to the reason that dwells equally in all persons. With this kind of understanding of Christ, no explanation exists for the Christian experience that Christ is uniquely able to redeem. Any great person, especially any rational person, could redeem. (Is it any surprise that this position tended to appeal to philosophers?) Now Schleiermacher is *not* trying to argue that Christ acted outside the bounds of reason; that stance would take him back to a super-naturalist position. But he *is* arguing that reason is not the absolute principle by which Christ redeems. As we shall see as we proceed, Schleiermacher identifies an awareness that precedes reason or conscious thought that is perfectly realized in Christ. Schleiermacher takes a path between super-naturalism and rationalism, distinguishing his understanding from both.

Schleiermacher's thought offers an openness to diverse doctrinal explanations of Christian faith, but an expectation that every explanation is open to critical examination and responds to objections with reasoned argument. Schleiermacher expected that this process of refining and reformulating our theological understanding will continue to be needed right up until the telos, the completion of creation.

Pause a moment to examine your reaction to that thought. Many of us desire more certainty than Schleiermacher allows us. As long as the process of theological understanding continues, the only certainty is that our doctrinal statements do not yet perfectly express faith.

How do you find yourself reacting to that claim?

Schleiermacher himself placed his sense of certainty not in his theology or his knowledge about God, but rather in his relationship to God through Christ, a relationship that he experienced to be deeper and more powerful than his understanding. From that place of certainty within a community of faith, he found himself able to respond positively to the existence of diverse doctrinal expressions.

Where does your certainty rest, and does it allow you to respond positively to different expressions within Christianity?

TYPICAL WAYS THAT SCHLEIERMACHER BUILDS AN ARGUMENT

One of the things that Schleiermacher does not do for us as readers is to separate out the few general statements he makes about Christian faith and doctrine from the particular statements that articulate his own view. The general statements are meant to apply to every expression of doctrine that can be accepted as Christian. For the most part, the propositions in *Christian Faith* are particular statements of his own articulation of doctrine. The general statements come up as part of the argument he makes in the elaboration of the propositions. A quick example we have seen before from §88 serves to illuminate the difference between the two kinds of statements. The proposition itself states Schleiermacher's particular view: "§88 In this collective life which goes back to the effectiveness of Jesus, redemption is brought about by him by virtue of the communication of his sinless perfection." He then proceeds to argue for this proposition by noting that it is not the only one current in the Protestant church. So he provides a general statement that names the boundaries for a Christian account of redemption, which must meet two criteria. First, every approach to blessedness must be traced back to Christ. Second, a community is formed in which nothing is sought to account for redemption beyond the influence of Christ and nothing is neglected that is part of his influence. Instead of emphasizing this general statement by making it a proposition in the doctrinal account, Schleiermacher uses the general statement in the course of an argument that both supports his account and allows for the possibility of other valid accounts. Most important for a beginning reader of *Christian Faith* to recognize is that the propositions are not general statements, but instead are a particular expression of one coherent system of doctrine. General statements provide boundaries but provide less specific content than particular statements. If you put all the general statements together, they would not make a coherent system of doctrine.

Another easy way to misunderstand Schleiermacher is to mistake a position that he is examining critically (and eventually will reject) and read it as if it were his own position. In the commentary that follows each proposition, Schleiermacher not only explains key aspects and implications of the proposition, he also contrasts his proposal with others and often shows the weakness of other proposals as a way of demonstrating the reasons his is preferable. If we as readers miss the signs that indicate that he is laying out something conditionally, we are sunk! The cue is usually a sentence that begins, "If then . . ." Because he understands that the perfect and final expression of Christian doctrine cannot be completed until the telos of creation is reached, Schleiermacher has to argue for why his proposed account is better than the others that are available. He cannot simply demand that he has hit upon the final true and perfect formulation. He shows both that his account is internally coherent and why it is preferable to others. *Christian Faith* is a carefully argued work and so requires close reading. Experienced theologians often read systematic theology like *Christian Faith* at only ten pages an hour! Grasping and evaluating an argument takes time. Why should we expect quick and easy reading? After all, we are trying to articulate that which is simultaneously at the center of our lives and at the very edges of our human ability to comprehend.

In light of this simultaneous being "at the center" and "at the very edge," Schleiermacher's approach to arguing a point may be very different from the way in which he first came to understand it, which shouldn't surprise readers. The argument follows logic rather than insight. We have looked at some of those moments of insight, such as the preaching metaphor, in order to help those of us who think metaphorically to understand the logic.

As all theologians must, Schleiermacher redefines terms as a part of his argument. Sometimes he redefines them explicitly and tells us what he does and does not mean when he uses a term. Sometimes we have to recognize the nuances that he gives a term by the way in which he uses it. A careful reader notices which terms are used frequently and begins to create a lexicon of how Schleiermacher uses those terms. By now you see that "redemption" is one of those terms, as is "God-consciousness."

One of the terms of logic that Schleiermacher uses is a particular source of confusion for readers who know anything about the work of the philosopher

Hegel, who was a younger colleague of Schleiermacher's at the university in Berlin. The term is "contrast," which seems innocuous enough. Schleiermacher uses the "contrast" between two poles to describe the entire range of possibilities that lies between them, which is somewhat like defining everything that is contained within a rubber band by pointing to the two outermost points of the rubber band. The contrast between those outer points defines everything held together between the points. This matter seems pretty obvious until we begin using it, as Schleiermacher does, to describe everything involved between two concepts. For instance, Schleiermacher uses the contrast between pleasure and pain to denote the whole range of human experience from pleasure to pain and everything in between (the bittersweet, for example). Hegel's use of such a contrast would be to show the tension between pleasure and pain and the search for a resolution of that tension that advances beyond them. Schleiermacher has no such idea of advancing beyond the contrasts he describes. Rather, Schleiermacher uses the contrasts to describe whole fields of human experience. For Schleiermacher, constrasts offer another way of describing diversity. Today we might be more accepting of a way of defining diversity that was not dualistic (pleasure or pain, black or white), but Schleiermacher was extending the dual poles to define and include everything in between, so he might agree with us and ask us to use our broader understanding when we come to the term "contrast" in his own work.

> Pause a moment to consider how you normally react to reading a carefully constructed argument. What can you do to strengthen your confidence as you approach Schleiermacher's argument?

We have prepared ourselves to think about Christ alongside Schleiermacher by noticing four things. His thinking about Christ is rooted in a deep relational faith. His book *Christian Faith* is limited in what it attempts to do; the book is a systematic presentation of one doctrinal account of Christ and does not presume to be the only Christian presentation of Christ. Schleiermacher embraces the diversity of expressions of Christian faith found in the community of faith. Finally, we examined typical ways that Schleiermacher organizes his thinking. The picture frame is in place. In the next chapter, we sit next to Schleiermacher and take a look at the reality he put on paper. We look at the experience of redemption itself.

3

Preparing for the Systematic Picture

Accounts of Redemption

THE HISTORICAL CONTEXT THAT DEMANDED
A NEW STARTING POINT FOR THEOLOGY

Typically in theology, innovative approaches to thinking through central beliefs are developed only in response to the emergence of problems that can't be resolved in the old way of explaining. The central beliefs used to interpret the person and work of Jesus Christ remained essentially unchanged for about a thousand years. By 800 C.E. the basic concepts used to interpret the Nicene Creed (325 C.E.) and the Chalcedonian Creed (451 C.E.) were widely accepted. Between 800 and 1800 C.E., they were almost unchanged. Not even the Reformation's profound reemphasis on grace changed the way the person and work of Jesus Christ were explained.

What happened, then, in the 1700s that pushed theologians and pastors such as Schleiermacher to find a new way to explain how Jesus could be and do what Christians experience through faith in him?

We still experience today the effects of the answer to this question. The power of reason was developed as a tool in natural sciences, social sciences, and history, which is not to say that before the 1700s thinking was unreasonable. Far from it! Rather, the scope of reason expanded. Reason had been understood to involve the use of logic and rhetoric (forms of convincing argument). Depending on the place from which one starts, almost anything can be proven using logic and rhetoric. They were the basic tools of theologians and other interpreters of the Bible. Then, in the 1700s, reason expanded to include what we might call "reasonableness." Something is reasonable if it is consistent with everyday human experience today. In the natural and social sciences, events that can be duplicated are considered reasonable. History doesn't duplicate itself, so the criterion is consistency with the laws of science and with common everyday experience. This expanded understanding of reason, which goes beyond logic to reasonableness, made possible an explosion of knowledge.

But think about what happens when the question of reasonableness is turned on the Bible, which in the 1700s occurred first on the Hebrew Bible. Scholars quickly concluded that many of the stories were legends or myths because events (such as the sun standing still to give Joshua time to win a battle) were inconsistent with human experience of the workings of the laws of nature. By the late 1700s, the miracles of Jesus and accounts of his birth and of his resurrection were also appearing unreasonable.

A new problem thus arose. Up to that moment in Christian history the Bible was unchallenged as a reliable account of historical events. The differences in accounts between various books of the Bible were recognized, but part of the task of biblical scholarship was to resolve any conflicts those differences generated. Using logic and rhetoric, the conflicts were resolved to the satisfaction of even scholarly Christians.

The criterion of reasonableness directly challenges the reliability of the Bible, as written, for use as a straightforward historical account of what happened. In the New Testament, the miracles and the birth and the resurrection of Jesus are unrepeated and unrepeatable events. By the criterion of reasonableness, we would have to judge such accounts of miracles as either exaggerations or as attempts to use mythic or symbolic language to describe a spiritual (rather than a physical) reality.

In the face of this challenge, two kinds of responses emerged: supernaturalist responses and rationalist responses. Both kinds of responses are still common in popular Christian comments today, and both kinds of responses still create problems for Christians when we explore their implications more thoroughly.

The super-naturalist responses to questions about the repeatability (and therefore the reasonableness) of Jesus' miracles, birth, and resurrection agree that they are unrepeatable. In fact, the super-naturalists argue, that is the very point! Jesus Christ was unique, one-of-a-kind: fully human *and* fully divine. Therefore, we ought to *expect* that what makes him special is beyond ordinary human experience. Jesus Christ was "super-natural," that is, outside the order of nature. As a consequence, repeatability is irrelevant when the question turns to Jesus. Repeatability cannot be used to judge his miracles, his birth, his resurrection, or anything else that has to do with his divine nature.

The problem with this super-naturalist distinction between what religious faith could say about Jesus and what reason could say was that it left Christians with less and less to talk about. On the one hand, discussing the humanity of Christ quickly became difficult because most of the activities of Jesus given emphasis in the New Testament were categorized as super-natural. On the other hand, scholars began to provide natural explanations for many of the miracles, so fewer features of the New Testament account fell into the undisputed realm of the super-natural. Finally, a necessary connection between a super-natural description of Christ and those of us living in the natural world became difficult to explain. Super-naturalist Christian thinking today tends to divide Christian thinking into two unrelated realms: religious thought and everyday secular thought. The desire for integration of these two realms pushed theologians to find an alternative to super-naturalist responses.

Rationalist responses fully embrace the criterion of reasonableness and apply it to the biblical accounts of Jesus. When they are finished, the powerful teachings and the death of Jesus remain. Jesus emerges as a moral leader who was willing to die for the truth of his teaching in the face of hostile civil and religious powers, making him one of many such leaders; Gandhi and Martin Luther King Jr. are familiar twentieth-century examples. In the 1700s, as this line of thinking was first being developed, rationalist theologians attempted to arrive at conclusions about Christ's place in the Trinity and other aspects of his divinity. The work of Immanuel Kant in his *Critique of Pure Reason* effectively ended the credibility of such efforts.[1] His later work, *Religion within the Limits of Reason Alone*, specified the limits of what could be said either about God or Christ using the tool of reason and reasonableness.[2]

The problem with the rationalist description of Christ and Christian faith is that such a description does not appear to account for the power of the biblical story. Nor does it account for the many dimensions of Christian faith that are unconnected to moral or ethical imperatives and action. Kant's major works were published in the 1780s while Schleiermacher was still in school. He read them and absorbed them. The challenge was to find an alternative to both super-naturalist and rationalist responses to reason. What in Christian faith is left out of both accounts?

Pause for a moment to bring to mind examples of super-naturalist and rationalist ideas that are still common in conversation about Christianity. Which kind of ideas do you hear more often?

What additional challenges face Christian thinking in the twenty-first century?

One example is the challenge raised in the late twentieth century: Is a white, male, middle-class image of Jesus sufficient to save and motivate oppressed peoples of color or women? Name some specific examples of this challenge.

Another example is raised in environmental theology: Can a means of salvation that is directed toward human beliefs and actions adequately account for God's concern for the whole creation?

What additional challenges can you identify?

Before proceeding to examine Schleiermacher's answer to the closing question in the text above, try answering it for yourself. What aspects of Christian faith in Christ are left out of both the super-naturalist and the rationalist accounts?

A REFLECTIVE ACCOUNT OF THE EXPERIENCE OF REDEMPTION THROUGH CHRIST

From Schleiermacher's perspective, we can see a number of aspects of Christian faith that are obscured or missing in the super-naturalist and rationalist accounts. Perhaps the most important point that is obscured is that doctrinal accounts of Christianity are argued from within the experience of redemption—that is, they start with faith experience of Christ. The super-naturalist and rationalist accounts both argue as if any observer, whether Christian or not, would come to the conclusion that Christ is the Redeemer. Super-naturalists argue on the basis of Christ's miraculous acts, including the resurrection, and rationalists argue on the basis of Christ's teaching. Both perspectives purport to be arguing objectively. What is obscured is that redemption is a subjective experience; it occurs within individuals in the context of a common community subjectivity that has a two-thousand-year history. One cannot prove to an outsider that Christ redeems; one can only hope to create conditions within which an outsider might experience redemption for himself or herself. Missing from earlier doctrinal accounts is acknowledgment of that basic insider starting point. Schleiermacher does not exclude the possibility of an objective account of Christian faith, but such an account is not a doctrinal account. An objective account might be created for apologetic purposes or perhaps to help provide church leaders with an accurate picture of the current state of the church. Doctrinal theology starts from inside the faith community's experience and shows implications of and connections between the different aspects of that experience.

What is the most basic testimony of Christians when speaking inside the faith community? "I owe it all to Christ." Schleiermacher thinks of what we owe to Christ not merely as a debt, but rather as a way of accounting for what has changed and what has become possible in our lives. Most especially, the hope that is ours has come to us as a gift through Christ. Christian hope is not readily explained by rationalist accounts of Christ. Schleiermacher makes the basic testimony that everything in Christian faith comes to us from God through Christ the touchstone for everything he says about all aspects of Christian faith.

Another feature missing or obscured in earlier accounts is that faith is relational. Through a relationship to Christ, we are brought into direct personal relationship to God. Both of those relationships are fostered in a community and are initiated by interpersonal relationships in which Christ's activity is made visible in the present day. Christian faith is more than concepts about God. Christian faith is a direct and intimate relationship that permeates all aspects of human awareness: intuition, emotion, thinking, and action. These aspects of human life are part of the "all" that Christians owe to Christ—both the relationship with God itself and all the ways that the relationship completely permeates our lives.

What has just been identified as a part of relationship with God is also obscured in the super-naturalist and rationalist accounts. That is, Christian faith includes emotional engagement at its core. Christians "know" themselves in the faith intuitively, emotionally, and conceptually—all three. No doctrine adequately represents Christian faith that does not account for this breadth of experience. A really well-conceived account will explain the place of intuition and emotion in the evocation and development of faith. For Schleiermacher, intuition involves receptivity to that which comes from beyond ourselves and a giving of ourselves to the moment of reception that leaves sorting out what we know and why we know it until later, after the moment is complete. Intuition is consciously allowing our awareness to be guided, shaped, or filled.

Having noticed which features of Christian experience Schleiermacher has made an effort to bring into an account of Christian faith, let us return to explore further the basic testimony.

What happened to us when we were redeemed? This question turns out to have a changing answer—even though we are only redeemed once! How can that be? Our redemption is so important to us that we keep reinterpreting it in light of our current thinking. We tend to explain what happened in terms that help us struggle with the growing edges of our lives right now, whether or not they are the same as the growing edges at the time we first became aware of our redemption. Redemption is a present reality, and we tend to interpret what happened in light of our current awareness, our current needs, and our current receptivity to divine action. Thus, the way in which we remember our redemption and interpret it depends both upon where our struggles were at the time of first awareness and where our struggles are now.

This description helps us understand why different explanations of redemption emerge among faithful Christians. It also can help us be more accepting of the changes in our own explanations of our relationship with God through Christ at different moments in our lives.

Let us examine three of the many different growing edges in life and the corresponding expression of what happened when we knew ourselves to be redeemed.

For all of us, at some point in our lives, the growing edge for us is developing self-control. We learn basic rules for living with ourselves and with each other. We develop our ability to exercise willpower and choose not to satisfy an immediate desire in order to keep the rules. Our reason for developing self-control is simple. We come to perceive that keeping the rules gives us something we want. For children, that "something" might be acceptance by parents, teachers, or peers. For an addict, that "something" might be freedom from the demands of the addiction (demand for money for drugs, for instance) or freedom from the consequences of the addiction (depression that follows from addiction to hopeless thinking, for instance).

When self-control is our growing edge, we experience redemption as providing the gift of the strength we need to make choices and providing immediate clarity about which choices are the right ones for us. We experience our faith as the source of the rules by which we need to live. We also experience Christ as the source of strength when we need to make choices. We talk about how Christ removes the big obstacles to our acting positively so that we are free to make the right decisions moment by moment. When we explain to ourselves how Christ does this, we turn to a cataclysmic event, an event big enough to equal the biggest, most deadly patterns of our lives. Usually we talk about Christ dying for us. Sometimes we say, "Christ died my death in sin so that I could live; his death set me free from death." If our growing edge is gaining self-control, those words are powerful for explaining our redemption.

But other growing edges appear at other times in our lives. If our growing edges are creating meaning and being productive with our lives, then we are more likely to desire ideals for living that encourage our unique creative gifts. We talk about the love of God shown in Christ as a guide for our lives. We want to know God's will for us and for our society so that we can do our part in it. Images of the kingdom or reign of God may be especially powerful for us.

When our growing edges are creating meaning, we experience our redemption as having given us a vision of love, justice, and community for our lives. We are raised with Christ and given a calling to fulfill. To ignore that calling is to return to a life in ignorance of our true being. As redeemed persons we are part of a divine plan that is bigger than we are and yet to which our lives contribute. We talk about the new life to which we are raised with Christ, and we measure our actions by Matthew 25:40—whatever you have done for the least of these, you have done for me.

Both of these growing edges lead us to forms of faith that are basically self-reliant. Once Christ removes the big obstacles, we expect ourselves to do what we're supposed to do. This self-reliance allows us to evaluate pretty clearly how we're doing; we know where we stand. We blow it, ask for forgiveness, and start again—whether we're struggling with addictions or building a more just society. The third growing edge involves letting go of this self-reliance.

Some persons experience a growing edge that leads to an intimate relationship with God which requires our complete trust rather than our knowledge of what God is doing with us or through us. Having at least developed habits of self-control and following a call that contributes to the kingdom of God, we find ourselves invited to trust God to guide us from within. This pattern is in contrast to expecting God to give orders that we are supposed to determine how to carry out using our best judgment and discernment. We are invited to release our need to be in control.

When complete and utter trust of God is our growing edge, we experience redemption as consciously having released control to God and developing a practiced openness to the guidance of God through our awareness, thoughts, emotions, and actions. Compare such an experience with how we experience redemption when our growing edge is developing self-mastery! While these experiences seem opposites, in fact, they are not. We cannot release control to God until we have pretty much mastered self-control first. We are likely to find that some aspects of our lives can be released to God quite easily and others are not ready to be released because we have not yet discovered their self-control. As we live on this growing edge, we discover that the greatest gift to us is the guiding of our attention that occurs in intimate openness with God. Frequently, this guidance occurs without our certainty about whence or from whom it comes. We learn to trustingly and quickly test if it is from God and to act on it if we don't receive a clear negative answer (i.e., this awareness arises from my own old "stuff," not from God). As a result of this negative form of testing, we frequently find ourselves acting when we aren't sure of whether the guidance is from God, which is precisely where the trust is developing.

Pause for a moment to think about your own growing edges. Do you see any similarities between your growing edges and the three that we have named?

What other growing edges have you or persons you know experienced?

How is redemption described by a Christian when one of these is that Christian's growing edge?

Finally, consider the growing edge of union with God. Can you begin to imagine yourself being one with God in ways similar to Christ's at-oneness with God? Schleiermacher's theology invites you to think carefully about what this might be like.

Now let's return for a moment to theological explanations of Christian faith. One theology cannot adequately explain all three of these experiences of redemption. Carefully chosen liturgical and poetic language can be evocative enough to express aspects of each experience simultaneously. That's a good thing! Such language allows us to come together in our worship. But when we are trying to be more precise in our reflection upon our faith experience— which is the goal of theology—we can achieve the most clarity if we focus on explaining from the viewpoint of only one growing edge.

Most theologians have worked from the viewpoint of the growing edge of self-control or the viewpoint of the growing edge of creating meaning. Schleiermacher works from the viewpoint of the growing edge of complete intimacy with God and union with God. Once we recognize this aspect of Schleiermacher's approach, we will be less surprised at how different his description is. Most of us resist thinking about faith in any terms other than those that help us deal with our own growing edges. Some of our difficulty with Schleiermacher may occur because his theology invites us to anticipate faith experience that we haven't had yet!

What is the hope that is ours through faith in Christ? To be made perfect as Christ is perfect, to use Pauline wording. Or in Johannine concepts, to be one with Christ just as Christ is one with the Father. Union with God is difficult to describe to a child or other concrete thinkers, so more physical descriptions of rewards are used to stretch toward the joy of union. Union with God simultaneously involves both loss of self and completion of each unique self. This union is the real Christian hope because we have already begun to experience the conditions for its fulfillment: freedom from sin and self-destruction in the form of forgiveness and a change of heart that makes possible exercising our wills in love toward God and toward all that is encompassed in the divine decree that yielded creation. In the face of signs in ourselves that we all too easily return to our former state, the hope that is ours in Christ generates an underlying joy and peace that is undisturbed by anything smaller than God. That same joy and peace are the signs to us of a new relationship to God.

This description gives a picture of a mature faith. The relationship is not an instrumental one in which we offer God certain things (faith, prayer, right action) and we receive things in return (protection, answered prayer). Children and concrete thinkers can conceive relationships only instrumentally. More mature relationships can be conceived as loving simply for the sake of the beloved, without requiring anything in return. Union with God involves a similar maturity of relational conceptualization. To imagine such a relationship is impossible for us until we are shown it, just as we rely upon seeing love that is unconditional before we can begin to imagine it or recognize it as a gift offered to us.

When we say, "I owe it all to Christ," one of the things we might mean, then, is that in Christ we see what union with God looks like and we can begin to imagine it as a possibility for ourselves. Our ability to recognize what God offers us arises from seeing Christ.

> Pause for a moment to try putting into your own words what you and your faith community experience as the hope to which Christ calls us. What do you mean when you say, "I owe it all to Christ"?

URBILDLICHKEIT

What we have said so far affirms that Christ evokes Christian hope but does not describe how. Such a description is never easy. The lyric, "Jesus, Jesus, Jesus, there's just something about that name," expresses both our confidence that Christ makes all the difference and our difficulty in choosing a word or words to express how.

We could say that Jesus Christ is a model for human life, especially for human life lived fully in relationship to God and to other humans. A model sets an ideal before us and demonstrates how the ideal is fulfilled. In the twenty-first century, a few athletes are models for training and performing their sport. They inspire us to greater effort. Models inspire, and perhaps they teach by example, but a model cannot give us an ability that we don't already recognize in ourselves. Models strengthen what is already within our awareness, which is why we choose them. The rationalists thought of Christ as a model for spiritual life. In their view, he taught and inspired greater moral effort.

But the aggregate experience of Christians across two millennia shows that Christ does more than teach and inspire our effort in living spiritually full lives. He does teach and he does inspire, but he also opens to us an ability for living in relationship with God that we did not even recognize that we had or could have. One of the familiar metaphors for the change that this opening of us makes says that we are no longer servants but are becoming children of God. We are not able to create that transformation in ourselves. We can be taught that it is true, but we don't experience it apart from a relationship to Christ. Many of us were taught as children that we are children of God, but the teaching was not enough for us to embrace the fullness of being adult children of God to which the metaphor points. Encounter with Christ opens the full possibility.

That actual encounter is mediated through persons in our lives who have themselves been transformed by and embraced Christ and the possibility of intimate connection with God. This connection is not a visionary revelation, but rather a person-to-person encounter with Christ as Christ is embraced and lives in persons in each generation. The chain goes back uninterrupted to the first disciples and to the historical Jesus himself. A careful reading of the Gospels makes clear that those first men and women who shared their days with Jesus were opened to embrace the same possibility and the same hope that we share today, which is why their stories are important to us. Their stories of encounter with Christ are the same as our own.

This description of Christ as more than a model shows Christ to be unique in our experience. No single English word expresses all that we have just attributed to Christ. No German word was available for Schleiermacher to use either, so he created one (which is easier to do in German than in English). To avoid confusion we'll use Schleiermacher's word: *Urbildlichkeit*. When Schleiermacher speaks of the *Urbildlichkeit* of Christ, he is referring to the effect that Christ has on those who encounter Christ, the transformation that opens the possibility of intimate relationship with God. Schleiermacher suggests that this capacity is not a feature of Christ's teaching or of anything else Christ did (including dying and rising from the dead). The effect Christ has is a result of his own perfectly realized intimate human relationship with God. Christ is the original, the first person in whom relationship with God is completely fulfilled. We see that in him, and in drawing us to desire to become like him, God opens the possibility for each of us as well. All of this comes to us as a gift when we encounter Christ. We do not do anything to make it happen. It is all an expression of the quality of Christ that Schleiermacher calls *Urbildlichkeit*.

Pause a moment. The most difficult thing in explaining Christian faith to ourselves and to others is describing how Christ evokes the hope that is ours. In the previous pause, you began to put into words the Christian hope as you and your faith community experience it. Look at what you said.

Now, try putting into your own words how you understand Christ evokes that particular hope. You might find that it helps you to formulate your answer to the related question: How does Christ save? Try writing that. However, many Christians discover that their explanation for how Christ saves does not fully account for their Christian hope. (Supernaturalist answers often demonstrate this problem, which is one of the reasons Schleiermacher sought a different kind of answer.)

OTHER OPTIONS FOR A STARTING POINT

Both the super-naturalists and the rationalists work within the Protestant principle of beginning with Scripture. They proceed to interpret Christian faith by interpreting the biblical text, and they do so in a way that can be replicated by others who start with the same assumptions. Thus, even the super-naturalists adopt an expanded concept of reason.

An obvious alternative option for a starting point is to let go of the principle of beginning with Scripture. The Roman Catholic and Orthodox theological traditions tend to turn first to the historic teaching of the church as it has interpreted both Scripture and creeds. This kind of approach assumes even an expanded concept of reason can yield false results unless it is guided by the wisdom of generations of Christian leaders who came before us. This beginning point relies on the slow and deliberate process of designated institutional leaders coming to interpretive judgments on behalf of all members.

For this beginning point to be credible to reflective Christians, the particular church institutions must have a history of reliability in matters of judgment. In Schleiermacher's context, this reliability had not been established. The Prussian Evangelical Church was formed by a merger of the Reformed Church and the Lutheran Church in the very years when Schleiermacher was writing the first edition of *Christian Faith*. The king, who had a small amount of theological training, made decisions about liturgy and other matters of church practice that many people in the church did not welcome. So in Schleiermacher's context, the institutional church had not established a history of reliability in matters of judgment. As a consequence, he developed the alternative starting point we have just explored—an articulation of the hope that Christ evokes in Christians.

Other possibilities for a starting point are also available. Remaining within the Protestant principle of beginning with Scripture, several different starting points have been explored since the 1700s. One of the facts about Jesus that has almost universal consensus among biblical scholars is that he was crucified in Jerusalem by Roman authorities. That fact can serve as a place from which to interpret Christian faith. The question to be answered is, Why would the death of one individual be the salvation of all who believe? A theory of atonement is usually used to answer the question. Atonement theories generally require us to assume some things about God that we have no way of confirming apart from direct revelation from God. In particular, they usually require us to assume that the offense that sin (however it is defined) makes against God may only be resolved by an action taken by God within the realm of creation. Explaining this concept based upon the biblical text is not simple because most of the biblical authors did not conceive the question in precisely these terms.

Another place to begin from within Scripture is with the distinctive Christian claims about Christ's resurrection. This approach is "reasonable" not because resurrection can be duplicated but because witnesses in the first century believed it had, in fact, happened. Note, however, the change we have just made in how we build an argument. The argument is no longer built upon the historical accuracy of the biblical text itself, but rather upon the faith of the early Christian community that is recorded in the text. If we are going to turn to faith, why not simply turn to the faith of Christians today, which can more easily be examined?

Yet another starting point is to seek the revealed Word of God that lies behind or within the words of the biblical text. If, after all, the act of God draws us to Christ and to redemption, then the definitive ideas about Christ should come directly from God. This starting point acknowledges that the biblical text itself is the work of Christians expressing as best they could their understanding of their faith. But God is behind that faith and the words of the text making God's action, God's Word, known through the frailty of human expression. This starting place allows us to embrace historically critical readings of the Bible and yet allows us to affirm divine certainty. But how are we certain? How do we recognize the Word behind the text? We have to rely upon the faith experience of the Christian community to have confidence that we have correctly identified that revealed Word. Once again we have returned to Schleiermacher's starting point: the shared faith experience of Christians in community.

As it turns out, all of the options for starting points for doctrine that attempt to avoid splitting our thinking into religious thought and everyday thought return to Schleiermacher's starting point. All of them begin with the Christian experience of redemption, even if they don't all acknowledge that starting point. But as long as we use our community's faith experience as the test for the reliability of a formulation of doctrine, we have, in fact, used it as our starting point.

Rather than the question "What have we experienced in redemption?" we have asked the question "What is our Christian hope?" What difference does our choice of question make? Hope draws our attention forward and maintains our awareness that we continue to be engaged in the process that began with our redemption. Although we can conceive of redemption as a one-time past event that is over and done, such a conception doesn't make very good sense of the process of becoming closer to God that the rest of our lives continue to seek and fulfill. Christian hope is always before us. It began in ways that we can identify, but it never lies behind us; Christian hope always lies before us and yet is already ours. When we begin with an account of our hope in Christ, we begin an account that will allow us to explain not just the beginning of our faith, but its entire journey to perfection.

WHAT DOES THIS ACCOUNT IMPLY?

We have an account of Christian experience of redemption and hope through Christ, but that account is not yet a doctrine or a systematic theology. We begin to move into developing such reflective theological positions by asking ourselves two questions: What stands in the way of humans having the experience we have described? What must be true of Christ in order for him to have the effect on us that we have named in our account of Christian experience of redemption and hope?

The first question—what stands in the way?—leads us to consider what Christians call "sin." The word "sin" is used in a variety of imprecise ways in everyday talk. We can achieve the greatest clarity for our theological understanding if we sidestep the everyday uses and ask our own question: What stands in the way of the experience of redemption and hope through Christ? If we think through that question carefully, then we'll have greater clarity for answering our second question.

What must be true about Christ, about who he is or was and what he does or did, in order for him to have the effect on us that he has? This question covers what is traditionally referred to as the person and work of Christ. We need a clearer understanding of what stands in the way in order for our answers to make fullest sense, so we can anticipate our answers only very briefly right now. To have the effect he has, Christ must have lived a fully human life like our own lives. Christ must have been a historical person, not a myth. Christ must have shown the real presence of God active in his life, and suffering and death must not have changed that active presence of God in Christ in any significant way. Those statements offer the basic implications of the account of Christian hope as Schleiermacher describes it. In the next two chapters, we explore why he saw those implications and how he filled in the details.

Pause a moment before turning to the next chapter. Put into your own words your answer to the question of what stands in the way of redemption and Christian hope.

What are the most difficult aspects for you to explain to yourself?

We have listed four implications of Schleiermacher's account of Christian hope.

Look again at your own account.

At this point, what implications do you see arising from your own account for who Christ is or was and what Christ does or did?

4

The Portrait's Theme

A Systematic Account of Redemption

We must start our exploration of Schleiermacher's systematic account of the experience of redemption by reminding ourselves that he is not trying to explain every experience of redemption through Christ. Instead, Schleiermacher is explaining redemption from the point of view of those Christians whose growing edge is letting go of willful control and allowing themselves to be led into union with God. For those of us who do not share this growing edge, his theological explanation invites us to consider the possibility that one day it might be one of our growing edges. For those of us who have been tempted to call ourselves contemplative, his theological explanation may evoke a sense of recognition that we had not anticipated from theology. In either case, we are embarking on a venture full of promise of greater understanding of intimacy with God, and for this reason we are likely to find ourselves strongly resisting it.[1]

In the previous chapter, we explored overall pictures of our experience of redemption. A dogmatic account works in the opposite direction, building toward an overall picture by carefully defining one detail of the whole at a time, even though each detail depends on all the others. To use a familiar idiom, in the last chapter we looked at the forest. Now we're going to focus on the individual trees. Certainly at some times dogmatic theology seems to "miss the forest for the trees," but taking the time to know the trees in the forest is time well spent, because different kinds of forests exist depending upon the kind of trees in them!

In this chapter, we examine redemption as an event from the viewpoint of developing intimate union with God. We examine what happens, why it happens, and how it happens. The answers to these three questions come from the definition Schleiermacher creates for three terms: redemption, sin, and communication. We focus our attention on these three terms so that in the next chapter we can be ready to explore what the definitions of these terms suggest must be true about Jesus Christ and his activity.

> Pause for a moment to note the way you define these three terms when you use each of them.
>
> A large portion of theology involves defining terms. The unique meanings that a theologian gives to the central terms in his or her theology usually contain his or her most significant ideas. When we start by recalling what *we* mean when we use a term, we find it easier to notice the special meaning that particular term has in someone else's theological system.
>
> When you use the word "sin," exactly what are you referring to?
>
> How do you define "redemption"?
>
> What happens when "communication" occurs?

Schleiermacher provides a one-sentence answer to the question of how it is that we experience redemption. In §88 of *Christian Faith*, he explains that redemption is brought about by Christ through communication of his sinless perfection. This communication continues in history up to the present through the community of the Christian faithful.

This one sentence uses all three key terms. When we understand it, we will have grasped the center of his theology.

SINLESS PERFECTION

The explanations that Schleiermacher provides for sin and redemption reverse the order in which we are used to thinking about them. The experience of redemption, for Schleiermacher, defines what is sin. Most of us were raised from the opposite point of view. We were told the rules, we broke at least some of them, knew ourselves to be "sinners," and then gratefully received release from those sins we had committed or might commit in the future. From this point of view, we know what sin is long before we experience redemption. Most of our attention is placed on what we are redeemed *from*: sin.

Notice that, in this familiar approach, the definition of sin comes from cultural norms, the rules we are taught. Some attempt is made in Christian cultures to use the sayings and teachings of Jesus as the basis for the rules, but most of them come from sources other than Jesus himself (such as the Ten

Commandments or rules derived by reason from natural law). In this approach, sin and its consequences are clear whether or not one has experienced redemption. One might choose to avoid sin simply because one's culture enforces consequences for engaging in acts that are defined as sinful. Redemption is release from some of the consequences of sins we have already accumulated and the power to keep the rules in the future.

In contrast to this familiar approach, Schleiermacher focuses on what we are redeemed *for*: intimate relationship, or communion, with God. In Schleiermacher's thought, everything is defined by what is coming into being rather than by what is left behind. Redemption is the development of Christ's God-consciousness within us. Sin is everything that limits or slows down the free development of that God-consciousness (§66.1). We cannot even become aware of sin until we have begun to experience redemption (§67). Until we know God-consciousness is possible, we cannot be aware of what prevents it from growing. Our awareness of sin, then, only comes with our awareness of grace. Grace comes first.

Notice that, in Schleiermacher's approach, establishing rules to define sin is difficult. Sin is not a thing in itself that a rule can identify. Sin is an absence of relationship with God and any diminishment of our relationship with God, however that might occur. Once we have received the grace of recognizing the possibility of intimate relationship with God, that knowledge cannot be taken away from us (§63.3); thus, at least a modicum of grace is always present in a Christian. At the same time, our relationship with God is never perfect either. Thus sin is also always present. Schleiermacher observes that grace and sin are both always modifying each other in Christians as our openness to intimate relationship with God grows and diminishes through the events of our lives (§63).

When saying that Christ has a sinless perfection, Schleiermacher is referring to the complete and utter openness to God that Christ has in every single moment, his God-consciousness. More specifically, he directs our attention to the way in which Christ allows God to guide his human awareness from within. Schleiermacher defines Christ's sinless perfection as the way in which "the lower powers of the soul," including Christ's senses and physical being, are receptive to impulses coming from his God-consciousness (§66.2). Christ's physical being is only an "organ" of his spirit, but physical being and spirit remain distinct agents. Recall to mind the metaphor we explored in chapter 1: preaching and saying more than we know or creating a work of art or literature by following where it leads. That metaphor points toward the quality of directed awareness that Schleiermacher calls Christ's God-consciousness— Christ's attention as it is directed by God toward people and objects and thoughts and feelings and sensations. The complete receptivity of Christ's God-consciousness in every moment is his sinless perfection.

In *Christian Faith*, Schleiermacher lays out the relationship between his definition of sin and many of the theological ideas about sin that have become part of Christian traditions. Schleiermacher has often been accused of having a weak view of sin and evil, one that does not clearly show what is right and what is wrong. Anticipating why readers might perceive him that way is easy. He provides no rules to follow, so persons whose growing edges require rules to aid them in making choices find Schleiermacher's thought of no help for them. He does not even provide principles by which to measure oneself and one's progress, or the progress of one's congregation or society. Intimate relationship with God does not lend itself to measurement. "How close am I to God today?" is an absurd question to try to answer when our intent is to be receptive in every moment. Simply asking the question distracts our attention from receptivity.

Schleiermacher takes great pains in *Christian Faith* to interpret Christian traditions to show consistency between his definition of sin and the insights contained in doctrines such as original sin (§68–§72). Those detailed explanations are not necessary for our understanding his Christology. What we need to focus on is the way sin is defined by our experience of redemption through Christ, rather than redemption being defined by our prior experience of sin. Sin is our awareness of all that limits our reception of Christ's God-consciousness.

COMMUNICATION

Let us turn now to the term "communication" in order to understand how Schleiermacher describes the process through which Christ's perfect God-consciousness becomes our own less-than-perfect God-consciousness. Schleiermacher says Christ brings about redemption through communication of his sinless perfection.

The term "communication" carries a number of different features, each of which is an important part of Schleiermacher's description of redemption. Schleiermacher is consistent with contemporary understandings of communication. Communication occurs (a) in a specific context (b) between two or more persons (c) who use particular techniques (d) to share content. We use these four aspects of communication to explore what Schleiermacher means when he says Christ communicates his sinless perfection.

The context for the communication of Christ's sinless perfection is always and only a community of faith (§113.1). The exact shape a community of faith takes will vary, but in some form that community is always the context. Such a community originates when persons recognize the overlap in each other's witness to faith through Christ (§113.1). A community of faith formed among the close followers of Christ even during his lifetime, and that community has continued to form in every generation of faithful persons since then. In the proposition immediately before the one in which he defines redemption, Schleiermacher says that Christians are aware that our experience of blessedness is grounded in a divinely effected overall life (§87). His terminology implies that this new life is a shared community.

So, in contrast to accounts we periodically hear of persons accepting Jesus as their savior as a result of reading the New Testament in an isolated prison cell, Schleiermacher defines communication so that it only happens in the context of a community of faith. Therefore redemption requires a community of faith. Schleiermacher goes so far as to say that were all Christians to disappear and someone should pick up the New Testament and read it, that person could not experience redemption (§100.1); for Schleiermacher, if only a text were required to communicate, then the incarnation of Jesus Christ would be unnecessary for redemption (§100.3). God could have provided the Scriptures and not bothered with incarnation (§108.5). The fact that God did bother with incarnation shows that interaction with a living person is necessary for redemption (§128.1).

In the context of a community of faith, interactions between persons that reflect Christ's sinless perfection do not appear magical or accidental. In the context of a community of faith, the reality of Christ's God-consciousness is visible as a pattern within and between the lives of the redeemed. The community of faith provides a context in which individual interactions illumine larger possibilities and support is provided for growing in grace—that is, for growing into Christ's relationship with God. Without this context, communication of the kind involved in redemption does not occur.

Communication of Christ's sinless perfection occurs between persons. Ideas do not require persons; we can encounter an idea through a book or film. But more than an idea is involved in this communication (§10, postscript). This communication—the possibility of a relationship with God like Christ's perfectly open and trusting relationship—grasps us, engaging our emotions, our desire, and our will to receive it (§88.3). Schleiermacher observes that if it took a person, Christ, to begin this communication, persons who are taken up with Christ into relationship with God are also needed to make such relationship visible as a possibility (§127.2).

So, to summarize thus far, in the context of a community of faith, persons who have been brought into intimate relationship with God through Christ make that possibility visible to others in the community. The implication is that, within a community of faith, some persons have fully experienced the beginning of relationship with God through Christ and some persons are present toward whom grace is directed preparatory to that relationship (§113.1). While this observation fits our experience of life in virtually every congregation, the observation is an uncomfortable one because it allows us to indulge in speculation about who in a congregation is where in the process. Schleiermacher avoids such speculation, first, by recalling that redemption includes a life-long process of sanctification (§110.1), and second, by recalling that redemption is not our achievement anyway, but a gift that we barely manage to keep from resisting. Without the support of a community of faith, we surely would have resisted allowing Christ's God-consciousness to become our own.

The particular techniques Schleiermacher recognizes as part of communication are only those that are a part of our everyday life—our words and our actions (§108.5). While he does not suggest that miracles are impossible, miracles or any other kind of direct supernatural intervention are not part of redemption. The only miracle is that a person with a perfectly sinless God-consciousness, Jesus Christ, came to adulthood in the context of an overall life of sin, that is, without benefit of a community of faith (§103.4). That point is the only one at which the supernatural enters in. Christ himself incorporates into the natural world by living that God-consciousness which was not yet part of the natural order. Having lived it, he has made it part of the natural order of human life, so no further intervention of the supernatural is necessary for redemption. Christ's preaching and his acts of steadfast love are sufficient to make plain the God-consciousness that guides his every moment. If Christ communicated only through ordinary words and actions and thereby redeemed his first followers, then nothing other than ordinary words and actions is necessary today. Redemption does not require magic. In fact, quite the opposite: redemption is the completion of human nature anticipated from the beginning of creation.

Finally, communication involves content; something is communicated. The specific content of the communication shared by Christ is the demonstration in his own human life that an intimate relationship with God in every moment is possible. Through what Christ shows us of himself, we catch a vision for ourselves in relationship with God. But the content is more than just a vision; included also is the power to live the vision (§100 and §108.1). Schleiermacher has already affirmed that redemption is entirely a gift of divine grace. We don't do anything to receive it, except not resist. God gives us the power to actually live in relationship with God in the course of the relationship itself. By initiating our intimate relationship with God, Christ is also communicating the power we need to live in it. The power is not separate from the relationship, but the power is more than the idea that relationship is possible. The actualizing of relationship with God is a communication of the power to live in the relationship, all of which begins with Christ.

REDEMPTION

Now we are ready to see how the term "redemption" in Schleiermacher's dogmatic exposition functions to summarize the central features of Christian experience.

Redemption refers first and last to the total effect that Jesus Christ has on persons who allow themselves to come under his influence. Everything included in the Christian experience of redemption can be traced to Christ (§11). Thus, redemption is not primarily about forgiveness of sin; that understanding of the effect of Christ is too narrow. Redemption is a transformation of human nature. Redemption begins to complete the creation of human nature by developing our God-consciousness, an intimacy with God in which God guides all of our awareness.

While this development is new from the human point of view, from God's point of view redemption is merely an effect of the single original divine decree that created the universe. From God's perspective, redemption is simply one effect of God's self-giving love.

Redemption occurs in the context of a community of faith, changing us from one life orientation to a new orientation, from being closed to God-consciousness to being open to God-consciousness. Such a change can neither be imagined nor supported apart from the companionship of others who have also been changed. After becoming oriented toward openness to God-consciousness, sin is experienced as a momentary interruption of that God-consciousness rather than as our regular state of being.

The change in orientation pervades our lives and our awareness; everything we sense, think, feel, or do is now potentially guided by awareness shaped by God. As a result, we cannot characterize the change by summarizing specific things that redeemed persons do or avoid doing. Redeemed persons are transformed from the inside out, not from the outside in. Our community of faith prevents us from being deceived by that fact or talking ourselves into claiming that our God-consciousness directs us to destructive self-indulgence.

Finally, "redemption" refers to a process. Within that process, other terms refer to specific moments. We identify those terms in detail in chapter 6, but for now, know that regeneration, conversion, justification, repentance, and faith each identify an aspect of the moment of transition from the collective life of sin to the collective life of grace. At that moment, misery or dissatisfaction is removed as the underlying experience of our lives. "Sanctification" describes our continued growth in the strength and unbrokenness of Christ's God-consciousness. This growth corresponds to an expanding experience of blessedness underlying our lives. All of these terms refer to aspects of the entire process of redemption. We may even say that the grace that prepares us for the moment of transition is also a part of the process of redemption (though preparatory grace is left behind at the moment of transition, whereas all of the aspects of that moment itself continue in the collective life of grace that has begun).

This definition of "redemption" is quite different from its use in other theologies and in everyday communication. We redeem coupons at the grocery store and an exchange occurs: so much off the price of an item in exchange for the coupon. Using this definition of the word, some theologies refer to redemption as the payment of Christ's life in exchange for the penalties we owe as consequences for our sin. These theologies not only use the term "redemption" differently than Schleiermacher, they also use the term "sin" differently. Sin in these theologies refers to specific transgressions rather than to the overall orientation of living without an intimate relationship with God.

What other differences do you notice between Schleiermacher's explanation and those that are familiar to you?

What questions would you ask Schleiermacher about his description; what points need clarification?

BLESSEDNESS

When we experience redemption we immediately experience blessedness. Intimacy with God is blessed, filled with an underlying joy that cannot be shaken. Thus we experience blessedness to the same degree that our God-consciousness has developed (§87.1). As our God-consciousness grows more constant, our joy grows more constant as well, which is our Christian hope; we experience approximation to its fulfillment in the present and we anticipate its completion.

The experience of blessedness occurs only in the context of the new collective life of grace that Christ initiates, which is to say two things. First, blessedness and all tastes of blessedness or approximations to it are only experienced in a community of faith. When Christ takes us into his God-consciousness by communicating his sinless perfection, he brings us into a community of faith. Consequently, blessedness is experienced in that collective life of grace that undergirds communities of faith. Second, in our life before redemption, in the collective life of sin or absence from an intimate relationship with God, no approximation to blessedness could remove that absence (§87). No attempt at a relationship with God that kept our distance, hedged our bet, or kept God outside our boundaries could remove the condition of the collective life of sin. Blessedness is the fruit of intimacy with God.

Blessedness is not the same as happiness multiplied moment by moment. Happiness depends on sensory or emotional stimuli to trigger it. Anyone can experience moments of happiness; we need neither God nor Christ to experience those moments. Blessedness has no stimulus. It is the gift of God that comes as a joy and confidence and sense of security that lie underneath and prior to our thinking and acting and feeling. Christ's sinless perfection is complete blessedness. As we assimilate more and more to his sinless perfection, our blessedness becomes complete also.

> Think of a time when you or someone you know has expressed a sense of blessedness. How was it different from feeling happy?
>
> Some other theological accounts emphasize our experience of struggle during our lifetimes ("here on earth") and define "blessedness" as the reward we will receive after our death because we endured the struggle. Under what circumstances would blessedness only after death be an attractive idea? What kind of actions would it encourage Christians to take?
>
> Under what circumstances would blessedness as the joy we have right now be an attractive idea? What kind of actions would a present joy encourage Christians to take, in contrast to the ones you just named?

KEY ASSUMPTIONS

Now that we understand what Schleiermacher means when he says that redemption is brought about by Christ through communication of his sinless perfection, we have grasped the center of his theological system. Before we fill in details about the person and work of Christ (in chapter 5) and about specific aspects of the moment of transition (in chapter 6), we should identify two key assumptions Schleiermacher has made.

The first assumption is that the experience of redemption is the same for us today as it was for the first followers of Christ. Schleiermacher assumes that the first followers experienced redemption through their relationship with Christ while he lived, taught, and moved about Galilee and Jerusalem. This theology is significantly different from many others. Schleiermacher's approach means that the death of Christ cannot play a decisive role in redemption, because if his death is necessary for redemption, then Christ's first followers could not have experienced redemption until he died or was resurrected. Since Schleiermacher reads the Gospels to show that his disciples recognized Christ as the Redeemer, they must have already experienced redemption through him prior to his death. An ancient theological tradition emphasized in Eastern Orthodox Christianity is that redemption began when Christ was born. Schleiermacher's assumption is consistent with that tradition. Encounter with Christ's God-consciousness is redeeming. His God-consciousness was complete at each stage of his development and was unbroken even by a tortured death on the cross.

The second assumption Schleiermacher makes is that creation is teleological, which is to say that creation is progressing through history toward completion as God intended. God is not fighting for control of creation, and creation is not headed for a cataclysm. God is in charge, and creation is moving toward fulfillment. Any evidence we might think points to the contrary is simply evidence of our denial both of who God is and of who we are and of the evil we can do when we are closed to God. No satanic power with a will of its own is fighting God and using us as pawns. That image is emotionally motivating, but not a description of reality. God is sovereign and no being exists to defy God, except ourselves. Schleiermacher embraces the vision from Revelation 21 as the telos, the end toward which creation is moving: a new heaven and a new earth. Yet he does not at the same time embrace the cataclysmic fight between good and evil forces described in Revelation 1–20. Schleiermacher assumes a very high vision of God; God is absolutely in charge.

Both of these assumptions have strong roots in Scripture and in the history of Christian theology.

Pause for a moment to think about your own theological assumptions. Identifying them for ourselves is not always easy. One of the times we notice them is when someone else's ideas contradict an assumption that is especially important to us. At what points have you found yourself reacting strongly or negatively to Schleiermacher's ideas?

How would you phrase what you understand to be the truth in contrast to what he says? Look carefully at what you have just said. Is it one of your basic assumptions?

PROOF, SUBSTANTIATION, AND WARRANT

Assumptions bring us to the problem of how we can claim a theological description is true. How does Schleiermacher prove that his account is actually how Christ redeems? No formal proof exists for the doctrine of redemption as Schleiermacher presents it (§88.1 and §100.3). A formal proof would work like a proof in mathematics; once one has accepted the premises, rules of logic alone shape the possible conclusions. Historical questions do not lend themselves to the methods of formal proof. Schleiermacher accepts the insights of the Enlightenment on this point, as did most theologians of his time and as do most theologians today. This acceptance was a change from medieval scholastic theology, which created precisely such formal proofs and ignored the dependence of Christianity on the historical particularity of Jesus. Reformation theologies created a different kind of proof, a proof from Scripture. The miracles of Jesus, as they are narrated in Scripture, were proof of his power to redeem, according to the Reformers. Note, though, that the connection is not clear between the powers described in those narrative accounts of miracles and the specific power to redeem. What is redemptive or redemptive-like in the miracles? Why, asks Schleiermacher, were not other miracle workers also redeemers? Scripture describes many miracle workers—Moses and Elijah the greatest among them (§103.4). But they were only considered prophets. The miracles narrated in Scripture thus do not directly prove that Jesus is the Redeemer. In fact, the miracles do not even clearly illuminate how redemption occurs.

Does this mean that as Christians we are unable to substantiate our account of our experience of Jesus as the one who redeems? Are we left in a relativism where anybody can claim and believe absolutely anything? Definitely not! A significant difference exists between an account that is substantiated and one that is simply opinion. While neither is a formal proof, a substantiated account offers a credible explanation of how it is truthful and consistent with human experience, including human religious experience. A substantiated account explains itself using the best insights available concerning human life and the natural order.

Schleiermacher provides a substantiated account of Jesus Christ redeeming through the communication of his sinless perfection. Schleiermacher says quite clearly in §88.1 that the explanation of redemption that he provides is not the only one possible. As we saw in the previous chapter, quite different explanations of redemption are to be expected, given the variety of viewpoints from which Christians remember and experience redemption.

A substantiated account of Christian faith shows how faith is consistent with cultural understandings of reality. But a substantiated account of Christian faith will not—Schleiermacher says "cannot"—convince us to trust Christ. The warrant for faith, the basis for trusting belief, is our experience of it. So we cannot prove or argue someone (including ourselves!) into faith. We can only attempt to help others experience what we have experienced in relationship with God through Christ. The only warrant for Christian faith that is possible or that is needed is the experience of being in relationship with God; nothing else is sufficient.

Most Christians would like our faith to be based on proof rather than on warrant. For those of us who can be satisfied with warrant for our faith (even if we secretly wish for more) Schleiermacher's account might be useful. For those of us who must have proof, Schleiermacher's account will be a disappointment.

Think of at least one person you know whose faith rests on proof. What is the strength of their faith? What are its limits?

Think of another person, one whose faith rests on warrant, and compare the strengths and limits of their faith with those of the first person.

5

Details of the Portrait

What Must Be True about Christ in Order for Him to Do What He Does?

Up to this point in our thinking about Christ, we have referred to Christ's God-consciousness as if we knew precisely what we were talking about. The metaphor of being a channel of something more in preaching that we identified in the first chapter helped us to do this with some confidence. But metaphors are most illuminating in theology if we use them as a tool to guide our exploration of a phenomenon. Having developed a dogmatic description of redemption as a whole, we are ready to think in great detail about Christ. Our metaphor can help us test the concepts created to describe what Christ did and who he was. The area of theology devoted to these questions is Christology, the study of Christ. Christology explores who Christ was (the person) and what he did (the work of Christ).

The ecumenical council of Chalcedon in 451 C.E. set the parameters for what Christians believe about the person of Christ.[1] The Definition that was hammered out makes a number of affirmations about what is true of Christ. The Definition, however, makes no attempt to explain how the affirmations can be understood all together. The challenge for all reflective Christians since then has been to work out in a theologically consistent way how apparently contradictory things can simultaneously be true.

The clearest example of the problem is the central affirmation about Christ—that he is fully human and fully divine. Generally we regard being divine as being unlimited and infinite—at least infinite in wisdom and love. How can someone who is infinite be a human being at the same time, since we all know humans are finite and limited? In every century, theologians have tried to explain how Christ is fully human and fully divine by using the

69

concepts of what it means to be human and what it means to be divine that are available in their cultures.

Schleiermacher did the same thing. He had some relatively new ideas available to him; the thinking about what we now call "psychology," the inner workings of the human mind and emotions, was just beginning to develop. In fact, Schleiermacher himself contributed significantly to the development of thinking about psychology in lectures he gave at the university in Berlin. He uses this thinking about how the inner life of human beings works as he thinks about how Christ is fully human and fully divine.

Schleiermacher does not start his thinking with the problem of describing the nature or natures of Christ. As we have seen, he begins by thinking about what we have experienced in redemption. This method allows him to approach the person of Christ from a different direction. He asks, What must be true about Christ in order for him to have the redeeming effect on us that he has? How could he possibly do what we know that he does: redeem us?

The results of his answers to these questions are the basis for his entire systematic account of Christian faith, the center of his theology. To see precisely how he thinks this concept through, we begin with his propositions concerning the work of Christ and then explore the person of Christ. This investigation leads us to his analysis of God-consciousness and human development. Then we look at the role that Christ's suffering and death plays in redemption. Finally, we analyze the differences between Schleiermacher's account of Christ and the results provided in twentieth-century historical Jesus research.

THE WORK AND THE PERSON
OF THE REDEEMER ARE ONE

What did Christ *do* that results in our redemption? He made his own inner life visible, a life in which every impulse was motivated by the divine will, a life in which his relationship with God took up, processed, and directed every physical input and every thought and action. In making his inner life visible, he evoked our receptivity to being taken up into that same relationship with God. Finally, he secured all those who are taken up into this relationship into a community, a physical presence for one another and for the world. The redeemed now experience blessedness.

In more traditional Christian language, Christ taught and preached regarding himself and the new relationships that his presence in the world established. He initiated the reign of God in a new life for individuals in community with him and with one another. He redeems the world from the collective life of sin and reconciles us to God. By establishing a new person in us, Christ eliminates the guilt for our former sin because the old life of sin has ended, and the new persons living in grace do not deserve punishment for that old life. Our joy cannot be shaken.

What we have just said in the last two paragraphs is all that we can know about the life of Christ and it is all that we need to know in order to experience redemption through Christ. Nothing else is necessary for Christian faith.

Of course, over the past two thousand years, Christians have used their imaginations to say many more things about Christ. After time, some of those things have come to seem absolutely essential to believe in order to be a "good Christian." One of the most important things Schleiermacher does in his theology is to change our focus back to relationships. Christian faith is not about what we believe; Christian faith is about our relationship with God. This relationship is patterned after the example of Christ. In fact, we come to trust that Christ draws us into the intimate quality of his own relationship with God, which also draws us into community with others who are trusting God. Very few beliefs are involved.

> Pause a moment to take in some implications of this account of Christian faith.
>
> How would you feel about your own faith relationships with Christ and with God if Schleiermacher is correct and very few beliefs are required?
>
> The early followers of Jesus did not have all the beliefs about him that later Christians imagined. They just came to trust that he was drawing them closer to God, who loved them dearly. Can you think of people in the Gospels whose faith is like your own? Schleiermacher's account implies that each of us probably can think of several!

One of the first implications of what we have said is that we cannot really separate what Christ does from who Christ is (§92). What Christ does is actually (1) to be the fulfillment of human being and (2) to help us to see who he is and what it means to be fully human (§93). The aspect of human being that was incomplete before the birth of Christ was an uninterrupted openness to God. Schleiermacher calls such openness our God-consciousness. As we observed in earlier chapters, our God-consciousness is not our thinking about God as if God were "out there" separate from us. The intimate relationship with God that we see in the person of Christ is one in which his relationship with God is such that every other aspect of his life is processed through that relationship. Schleiermacher makes this point by saying that all aspects of Christ's life were taken up into Christ's God-consciousness.

Let's explore this concept in greater detail. All fully functioning adults process everything that happens to them through thinking and intellect. We take in physical sensations as well as emotions and determine whether or not to act in response to each of them. Because we are able to decide how we will respond, we are considered responsible for our actions. Even when we do not actually think before we act, we are capable of doing so and we hold ourselves responsible when we do not. Except for involuntary reactions (like throwing up our hands to block something that comes flying at us), everything is processed through our thinking, or could be.

What we see in Christ is an additional level of processing that is possible, one that we may not have been aware of in ourselves but that we recognize because Christ always uses it. At this level, not only our emotions and physical sensations are taken up and processed, but so is our thinking. This level is our relationship with God.

Where is this level located in our psychological makeup if it can guide even our thinking? Schleiermacher describes it as follows: every stimulus that comes to us, whether it comes from outside us or from within us (our feelings, our physical sensations), is translated by us either into a thought or an action (§3). For instance, an errant ball comes flying toward our face and either we think "a ball!" or we duck without even thinking. Sometimes we process something first as a thought, and then the thought leads to action. In Schleiermacher's picture of how we function, everything is processed immediately either as a thought or an action, but Schleiermacher points to a moment before that transition is made to either thought or action. Our immediate awareness occurs in the split second *before* we translate a stirring into a thought or an action. This idea is not easy to grasp because it stretches us not just to observe ourselves thinking, but to observe that something happens within us when we are not thinking. He is inviting us to observe the awareness we have *before* we think. Our immediate awareness is the location referred to by his technical use of the word "feeling."

In that immediate awareness before thinking or acting, we sense that things outside of us influence us and that we influence them in return, even if slightly. We depend on them and they depend on us. The other cars on the road, the food we eat, all the features of our culture—in our immediate awareness, we sense that we influence them, even if only by our presence, as well as being influenced by them. Schleiermacher observes that, in our immediate awareness, we also sense that one being influences us whom we do not influence in return (§4). We are utterly dependent on that one. In Christianity, we learn to call that one "God." So in our immediate awareness in every moment of being stirred by something, before thought about what has stirred us, we sense a relationship with God who influences us but whom we do not influence in return. God's influence is upon that immediate awareness that precedes every thought or action.

What we have just said describes the psychological makeup of every human being, according to Schleiermacher. The influence of God is upon the immediate awareness of every human being. What differentiates us is how frequently we translate that influence on our immediate awareness into our thoughts and actions. Some of us don't translate God's influence on our immediate awareness into *any* thought or action. At the other end of the spectrum, Christ translated the influence of God in his immediate awareness into *every* thought and action. Schleiermacher does not mean to imply that God was whispering into his ear and telling Christ what to think and do. Then Christ would be thinking directly rather than receiving the influence of God in the moment *before* thought. Christ in that case would have been a puppet rather than a human being. Instead, Christ is just like us—except that he was able to do perfectly what we didn't know we could do at all until we experienced redemption. He was able to translate the influence of God on his immediate awareness into every thought and every act of his entire life. That translation of his immediate awareness of the influence of God into thought and action is what we have been calling his perfect "God-consciousness." Using observations about the working of our minds, Schleiermacher has given us a way to think about how a human being can be aware of God in every moment while living in the midst of ordinary life.

Have you ever tried thinking before about how God communicated with Christ? Most of us assume that Christ just heard a voice in his mind telling him what to do. Of course, it follows that if we do not hear such a voice, or we can't determine if we are just hearing the voice of our own desires, then we could not possibly be like Christ in any way. Schleiermacher is suggesting that we are exactly like Christ because we also can translate the influence of God on our immediate awareness into our thoughts and our actions. We have old habits of thinking and acting that we have to break and so we're not as consistent at doing this as Christ was, but we are growing in our consistency. In this manner, Schleiermacher suggests that we think about the biblical injunction to "have the mind that was in Christ." For those whose growing edges are uniting with God, this approach probably sounds wonderfully hopeful. How would it sound to those whose growing edges are self-mastery or those whose growing edges are creating meaning and purpose?

Notice one implication of what we have said so far. Because our immediate awareness comes *before* our thinking and our acting, we cannot change how that immediate awareness translates stirrings into thoughts. Our only ability to change things comes through thought itself, which means it comes *after* the translation is already made. Thus we must conclude that any change we experience in translation of our immediate awareness must be a result of the influence of God. In other words, the changes that come as part of our redemption are a gift of God's grace and not our own acts. We can resist them or be open to them, but we can't make them happen.

We return, then, to what Christ does that results in our redemption. He makes visible the influence of God on his immediate awareness and his translation of that influence into every thought and act; in other words, he makes visible his perfect God-consciousness. When we see that in Christ, we are drawn to it and become receptive to the same influence of God in ourselves. Christ thus evokes our response to him and to God through his teaching and preaching about himself. If he were not the fulfillment of human being, then his teaching could not have the power to redeem. Because of who he is in relationship with God, his teaching is about himself and has the power to evoke our receptivity to God's influence (§93). Otherwise, his teaching would only be moral guidance for what we ourselves would try to accomplish but could not achieve; that is Schleiermacher's response to those who rank Jesus as one of the great moral teachers of the world. If we could be moral by our own willpower and being moral is attractive to us, why aren't more of us moral? Schleiermacher concludes that Christ must do more than teach about how to live; Christ must teach about what he himself embodies in a new kind of relationship with God.

The difficulty we have just experienced in trying to put into words an immediate awareness that comes before words and thought makes it clear why the community of faith is so important. We catch a vision of the possibility of translating our immediate awareness of the presence of God into our thoughts and actions by seeing someone else actually doing it. Then, after redemption, we aren't able to be consistent in our own immediate awareness of the presence of God, let alone in our translating it into our thoughts and actions. So we need the community of faith for encouragement and reassurance in the face of the strength of our old habits that obscure the presence of God. (Schleiermacher identified those habits as what constitutes the old life of sin.)

TESTING THE CONCEPTS

Now that we have the concepts in mind, let us test their usefulness by seeing how adequately they describe and explain what occurs in the experience of preaching or of creating that we identified in the first chapter as a metaphor for our God-consciousness. Recall what we said about those experiences: we are open to God or at least to something beyond ourselves even while we are concentrating on the congregation or the medium in front of us, and we discover when we look back at the experience that we have said or created something more than we knew consciously. How do Schleiermacher's concepts of immediate awareness and sensing the presence of God in our immediate awareness interpret this experience? In those experiences we have described, our imme-diate awareness is very open to the influence of God. Because of that influence we are able to translate our sense of the presence of God into thought and action more completely than we normally do. The process is entirely human, but we're better at it than we usually are. We are still very much ourselves, and yet we are more effectively translating our sense of God's presence from our immediate awareness. Because the translation is happening, others can glimpse the presence of God in us in our words and actions in those moments.

> Pause for a moment and think through the experience you identified from your own life that is like the preaching or creating experiences of others. How do the concepts proposed by Schleiermacher apply to your own experience? Where do the concepts do a good job of describing your own experience, and where do the concepts create puzzlement or fall short?

For many Christians the concepts work pretty well to account for our expe-rience. They make it possible for us to extend from our experience of those fleeting moments to imagine how Christ could translate his sense of the pres-ence of God in his immediate awareness in every single moment of his life. Schleiermacher's account of Christ says that this awareness is precisely what it means to say that the being of God was in Christ (§96.3). Once we have expe-rienced redemption through him, the difference between Christ and ourselves is one of degree; he is perfect at translating his sense of the presence of God in his immediate awareness and we are not. The difference between Christ and ourselves is not a difference of kind, meaning he would have a capacity or a quality that we do not have at all. He is like us in all things excepting sin, says the Chalcedonian Creed. In other words, he is like us in all things except that his translation into thought and action of his sense of the presence of God in his immediate awareness is perfect and unbroken and our translation is imper-fect and frequently interrupted. The implication here is that God is present to us in exactly the same way as God was present to Christ. Redemption allows us to respond to that presence of God in the same way that Christ did, though less consistently because of all the old habits of thought and action that interfere.

GROWTH AND DEVELOPMENT IN CHRIST

The nature of theologians is to think about things we know or have figured out and then to ask ourselves additional questions. The solution to one set of difficulties in theological accounts always creates another, different difficulty.

We tend to prefer theological accounts in which the difficulties bother us the least. We should expect to find some loose ends to ponder in Schleiermacher's theological account, even if we find it extremely useful for explaining and supporting our faith experience.

One of the questions that might well occur to us at this point is to ask how Christ's openness to God was expressed before he reached mature adulthood. Was he perfect once he reached maturity, or can we understand in some way that he was perfect even in his infancy and childhood while his thoughts and actions were limited by the capabilities of an infant or a child?

Schleiermacher's answer to this question is probably not as nuanced as we would like it to be. The field of developmental psychology did not yet exist with all of its careful observations of the changes in what newborns, infants, and children perceive and process with their growing minds. In fact, the idea that human capabilities change and expand was a new concept in the half century before Schleiermacher started thinking about human nature and Christ. Schleiermacher observed the development of human capabilities in his own children and in parishioners and students he taught. His account of Christ reflects these observations. If Christ was fully human, then his capabilities for thought and action must have developed from his infancy through his adulthood. But Schleiermacher also affirms that Christ's God-consciousness was perfect throughout his entire life, from birth to death (§97.2). So did Christ's God-consciousness grow and develop? Or was his sense of God's presence in his immediate awareness always the same, and all that changed was how it was translated into thought and action? That is, was his sense of God's presence translated into the thoughts and actions of which an infant is capable, of which a child is capable, and finally of which a mature adult is capable? Schleiermacher did not have the concepts available to him from developmental psychology to sort out which of these alternatives best fits with his account of Christ. For this reason, his account leaves the question open. What he is sure about, however, is that Christ developed in the way that has come to be identified as normal for human beings to grow from infancy into maturity. He must be sure about that, otherwise Christ was not fully human.

Which way of explaining Christ's development do you think best fits both Schleiermacher's account of Christian faith and the understanding of human development that we have today? Have you thought about how relationship with God is experienced by a one-day-old infant? If Schleiermacher is right and faith is neither a thought nor an action, then we would expect that even an infant that young has a relationship with God. Try describing for yourself how an infant experiences faith.

What does this discussion indicate to those of us who don't want to think in such detail? Our relationship with God is not primarily something that we believe—that is, it is not located in our thinking. And our relationship with God is not primarily a set of things that we do—that is, it is not located in our actions. Our relationship with God involves a willingness on our part to acknowledge our utter dependence on God, and further an awakening of our ability to process *everything* through openness to the influence of God. This openness is actually trusting that God guides our thoughts, our emotions, and our actions to the extent that we allow. A community of faith is needed to affirm for us as individuals that God's influence is evident in our lives, especially when we have not been aware of that influence in our thinking.

The answers to two very common self-doubts among Christians are implied here. Does a "good" Christian need to know how to pray in a particular way? Implied in Schleiermacher's account of Christ is a clear "no!" Faith —including prayer—is not an action. Faith is openness to God in our immediate awareness, which is translated into thoughts and actions of various kinds. No one kind of thought or kind of act (including prayer) expresses faith. The very fact that we desire to be open to God is an indication that we have experienced redemption through Christ, since only Christ can evoke that desire in us and what we desire is actually to participate in Christ's openness to God. Every thought and every action of Christ translated his sense of the presence of God in his immediate awareness, so no single thought or action is "right" while all others are "wrong." And consequently, no prayer thoughts are guaranteed to be "right" while other prayer thoughts are "wrong." Christ's thoughts included joy, sorrow, compassion, and anger. He does not demonstrate only one correct way to pray. To desire to be open to God and to speak our minds and hearts in whatever way the sense of God's presence in our immediate awareness translates itself is quite enough.

A second common question is similar: Does God judge me to be lacking? Schleiermacher's answer changes the question. God determined to lavish the gift of redemption through Christ on each of us. We must have been lacking in order to need the gift in the first place, but that lack has become irrelevant. What God sees is Christ in us. That is, God sees us growing in the God-consciousness that is also Christ's God-consciousness. God knows that we desire that growth and are resisting all the old habits that impair our ability to translate into thought and action our sense of the presence of God in our immediate awareness. We are new people even though we are not yet the people that we desire to become, and that change is what God has given us in Christ; it is enough!

Most of us would prefer to be more in control of the relationship ourselves; we would like to be able to identify something in what we believe or in what we do that is evidence that we are "on the right side" and safe. Living with Schleiermacher's account of Christian faith requires us to acknowledge that we live primarily in trust rather than with sure knowledge that we are safe. Faith is not our possession; it is a gift we receive moment by moment. Even our best theological thinking cannot replace our trust.

> Most Christians venture into theological thinking because we hope that it will provide us some answers and by providing answers will relieve us of some of the anxiety that comes with trusting God so much. Many theological accounts oblige this desire and offer more certainty than Schleiermacher does. Do you see the trust that runs throughout Schleiermacher's account as an asset or as a liability to encouraging the faith of Christians? Why?

THE SUFFERING OF CHRIST

For the sake of moving forward, let us assume that we have decided that we find Schleiermacher's account of Christian faith helpful up to this point. At least two major questions are sure to have occurred to us by now. The suffering and death of Christ on the cross has not been discussed at all. What role does it play in redemption? Second, Schleiermacher seems to be projecting our faith in Christ back onto the historical Jesus. What is the relationship between the first-century Jesus and this picture of Christ?

In the theological accounts of Christ that are familiar to most Christians, the suffering of Christ on the cross is the act that redeems us. Schleiermacher rejects this approach to explaining redemption because in it nothing new or unique that Christ embodies fulfills human nature. If Christ accepts the punishment for our sin, we are left unchanged; we still deserve punishment. We have no hope of avoiding sin in the future because we are the same old people with the same old habits that interrupt our relationship with God. In Schleiermacher's view, this account does not explain how redemption transforms us nor our experience of blessedness. The understanding in the account that Christ is the Son of God explains how one person's suffering might cover the whole human race's punishment, but does not explain how we are transformed at all. This life holds no hope if redemption does not transform us, which explains so much emphasis on life in a world to come in other theologies. Schleiermacher observes himself and other Christians experiencing hope in this life as a result of redemption. We are already blessed.

If Christ's suffering is not what redeems us, why did he suffer and what can we learn from it? Christ suffered because everyone who lives in the collective life of sin is subject to suffering. Consequences flow from the habits that interrupt our openness to relationship with God. Sometimes the consequences do not fall upon the person who has sinned; sometimes they fall on persons close to them, and sometimes on persons far away. We observe this phenomenon quite often. The inability of parents to compromise their own desires has consequences for their children; the inability of factories to avoid polluting the air affects persons hundreds of miles away. The consequences of sin do not fall just on the sinner. This reality allows us to recognize that Christ, who was sinless, nevertheless experienced the consequences of the sin of the collective life in which he lived. He suffered as a result of sin.

This observation leads to two conclusions. The first is that blessedness, which is experienced as a result of utter openness to God through redemption, does not have to be disturbed just because one lives in the midst of a culture in which sin is the norm. Christ lived among sinners, and the suffering he experienced did not disturb his blessedness. While he did not choose the cross for himself, his blessedness was not even broken by that amount of horrible suffering. We see as a result of Christ's suffering on the cross that nothing interfered with his perfect God-consciousness, and so we have a clear picture of the power of the connection with God that is possible for redeemed human beings who are taken up into his God-consciousness.

Two counterexamples from the Gospels probably come to mind at this point. Matthew and Mark both record Christ crying out from the cross, "My God, my God, why have you forsaken me?" This exclamation sounds like a loss of connection. In his lectures on the life of Jesus, Schleiermacher observes that this statement is the opening line of Psalm 22 and that the psalm ends with a strong affirmation of trust and connection with God. The psalm also duplicates much of the physical experience of Christ on the cross. So Schleiermacher concludes that Christ had in mind the entire psalm when he spoke the opening line, and so the quote does not at all indicate that Christ felt cut off from God for even a moment.[2] Some scholars of the Gospels today dismiss the historicity of the quote as words spoken by Jesus and conclude that the author of the Gospel of Mark selected Psalm 22 and placed it in Jesus' mouth, and then Matthew simply quoted Mark. Regardless of which explanation one prefers, if one does not find a satisfactory explanation for the presence of the quote in Matthew and Mark, then the quote directly challenges Schleiermacher's entire account of Christ's God-consciousness and of what we experience in redemption through Christ.

The second counterexample is less difficult for Schleiermacher to defuse in his own mind. The Gospels portray Christ expressing deep grief, particularly in his prayer in Gethsemane and in his weeping over Jerusalem. We might find it credible that our sense of the presence of God in our immediate awareness could translate into grief, especially when what is stirring our immediate

awareness is suffering. Schleiermacher was not comfortable with this explanation, however. He explained the grief recorded in the Gospels as fleeting
moments that do not change our overall impression of Christ's blessedness
accompanying his perfect God-consciousness.

> These two counterexamples are the ones Schleiermacher himself identifies and to which he
> responds. Are there other examples that you can identify from the Gospels that seem incon-
> gruous with Schleiermacher's picture of the God-consciousness of Christ?

We can draw a second conclusion from the observation that Christ experienced suffering as a result of living in the midst of the collective life of sin.
Christ's life in our midst was an expression of God's love. Christ did not ever
experience disconnection from God himself, but he willingly experienced the
consequences resulting from that disconnection, the consequences of sin, by
living in our midst. So when we refer to the suffering of Christ, we have in mind
what he experienced throughout his entire life, not simply what he experienced
on the cross. The decision to live in the midst of a suffering world in order to
redeem us by his presence is redemptive, not the suffering of Christ itself.

> One of the advantages of this way of thinking about Christ's experience of suffering is that
> we are not encouraged to seek out experiences of suffering in order to imitate Christ. Still
> less can we justify requiring others to suffer. The history of Christianity has many examples
> of persons with power claiming that those who suffered at their hands were fortunate
> because they were imitating Christ (willingly or unwillingly). Can you think of one such
> example from Christian history? Have you seen this happen in your own experience?

HISTORICAL JESUS RESEARCH
AND FAITH THROUGH CHRIST

In Schleiermacher's observation and account of Christian faith, faith clearly
does not rely upon history for proof of its power or its truth. Faith is based
upon our experience of living in it, not upon a historical account. Faith is
evoked by glimpsing the God-consciousness of Christ effecting the words and
actions of Christians in the community of faith. When we are taken up into
that God-consciousness ourselves, we know its power and its truth. Our experience provides all the confirmation that is needed or possible.

Having made this point, is it possible that Christ is only a myth and that the
first-century person named Jesus from Nazareth was entirely different from the

Christ whose God-consciousness we encounter in faith? Just one year after Schleiermacher died, David Friedrich Strauss made this argument quite force-fully.[3] Strauss concluded that no connection existed between the first-century Jesus and the Christ of faith. One very significant assumption about Christian faith lies behind Strauss's careful historical reading of the New Testament. That same assumption is embodied in the first criterion for determining whether an idea or an account found in the New Testament was created by the early churches or whether it goes back to Jesus himself—a criterion that historians still use today. The assumption is that the death or the resurrection of Jesus was decisive in form-ing Christian faith. That is, prior to Jesus's death or resurrection, his first fol-lowers had a different experience and understanding of faith. If one holds this assumption, then clearly everything that belongs to Christian faith in Christ today is probably different from Jesus's own understanding of himself. This con-clusion is the basis for the criterion that nothing that is attributed to Jesus in the New Testament but which is consistent with Christian faith after his resurrection can be considered reliable historical information about Jesus's life. Christians likely projected their faith back onto Jesus's life and added details and stories that "could have happened" from their perspective but did not actually occur.

Historians generally do not recognize, even today, that one of their criteria for historical judgments rests upon a theological assumption about how redemption occurs. Their assumption creates a problem that Schleiermacher did not have. As we have seen, Schleiermacher's account of redemption assumes complete continuity between the faith experience of Jesus' followers during his lifetime and their faith experience (and ours) following his resurrection. Jesus' death causes no change in faith relations nor any change in an under-standing of what has happened. So Schleiermacher does not *have* to rule out all sayings attributed to Jesus that are consistent with the faith understanding of later Christians. He does rule out some sayings for other historical reasons; he does not take every word attributed to Jesus as an accurate historical record. But based upon Schleiermacher's understanding of redemption, faith coheres with an accurate history of the life of Jesus.

Schleiermacher, however, still approaches the Gospels using critical tools and questions. The Gospels as they are written do not provide an accurate his-tory, in his view. Critical reading of the texts in light of historical evidence from other sources is essential. These sources would include reports about Jesus from his opponents, if we had them.[4] Sources also include other literature from the time and archaeological evidence. Biblical scholars today use these same sources.

Schleiermacher tended to take a larger view than historians do today. Accounts of the "historical Jesus" these days only use evidence that comes from first-century Palestine. Consequently, both the outer events and the inner life of the man can be described only to the extent that they were understood by the people who wrote the sources in the first century. In Schleiermacher's view, these sources do not adequately account for the full experience of Christ that we have today. If the source of our sense of God's presence in our immediate awareness is not the first-century man named Jesus, where did it come from? If not from Jesus, then we should be centering our faith around some other individual and not around him. For Schleiermacher, the historical Jesus is not just what can be said about the man from first-century sources; the historical Jesus is also the one whose influence has been felt throughout history since his life on earth. A historical account of Jesus is incomplete if it does not include a means of explaining the nature and extent of his influence throughout history.[5] Because of Schleiermacher's understanding of the way redemption occurs through the communication of a perfect God-consciousness, conceiving that the influence of Christ could be based on anything other than features of the actual first-century man is not possible. Redemption does not happen through hearing about the man (in which case stories could be made up about him and those stories could be the basis of faith); redemption occurs through encountering the God-consciousness itself, passed on from person to person all the way back to the first person to embody it: Jesus Christ.

This point is critical in thinking through your own Christology. Schleiermacher is often accused of not being a real historian because other historians think that he reads his faith back onto history. Consider two basic options and some of the historical questions each of them has to resolve:

1. If you think that redemption occurs because of Jesus' death or because of his resurrection, then you are likely to agree with those historians. Why does any historical information about the life of Jesus matter then to Christian faith? Why not be like the apostle Paul and simply preach Christ crucified and nothing more (no Christmas, no parables, no miracles, etc.)? Must the life of the first-century Jesus be consistent with Christian faith after the resurrection? The connection between most of the historical reconstructions of Jesus' life made by historians today and the faith in Christ that has developed in the church is difficult to see. Where did the faith we have today come from, if it cannot be traced back to the life of the first-century Jesus? Is it "true" faith if it did not come from Jesus himself?

2. If you agree with Schleiermacher that redemption is communicated from person to person across the generations all the way back to Jesus' lifetime, how do you account for the emphasis on his death and resurrection that has arisen in Christian faith? For instance, why did the apostle Paul preach both that the power of death is broken by Jesus' death and that Christ was the second Adam, the perfection of human nature in relationship with God? If Christ being the perfection of human nature was so important to Paul, why did he never give any of the details of Christ's life in his letters?

Take some time to think about these questions. The difficulty you have in answering some of them will help you discern why you prefer one explanation instead of the other.

We have now clarified Schleiermacher's account of the three major themes in Christology: the work of Christ, the person of Christ, and the connection between Christ and the historical record about Jesus of Nazareth.

Christians with different growing edges tend to prefer emphases other than Schleiermacher's. Persons whose growing edges involve self-mastery tend to emphasize the divine nature of the person of Christ and the miraculous, expectation-breaking, life-changing aspects of his work. Persons whose growing edges involve generating meaning and living out a vocation as one's purpose tend to emphasize the humanity of the person of Christ, his proclamation of the reign of God, and his forming a radically new community—indicating that the reign of God is already present—as his work.

Schleiermacher was aware of these differences among Christians in his congregations, especially the one in Berlin. His preaching always presented Christ as the Redeemer who makes possible our own uniting with God. He consistently explored the dimensions of living in intimate relationship with God through Christ as an invitation to experience it. This systematic theology will "preach," because it invites us all to grow in grace.

6

Other Features of the Picture

Classic Terms, Biblical Stories, and the Doctrine of the Trinity

Chapter 4 presented the theme of the big picture by clarifying what Schleiermacher means when he says that redemption is brought about by Christ through communication of his sinless perfection. Schleiermacher uses common terms from Christian thought to identify details in this process, but no single standard exists for the specific meaning of the terms he uses (regeneration, sanctification, justification, conversion, repentance, faith, regret, change of heart, preparatory grace). This lack of a standard requires us to learn to use these terms with Schleiermacher's interpretation of them in order to understand his picture of redemption in its richness and subtlety.

DEFINITION OF CLASSIC TERMS

A diagram of the relationship between some of the terms starts our discussion.

Preparatory grace → Regeneration → Sanctification
Collective life of sin   Transition   Collective life in grace

Regeneration is the transition between the collective life of sin and the collective life in grace (§106.1). Schleiermacher is intentionally vague about whether regeneration happens in a moment of sudden change over a period of time. He is trying to avoid making one version of Christian experience the standard by which everyone is expected to judge themselves. Some of us can name a date and a place where the transition occurred—a revival or a prayer meeting. Others of us can only look back and say, "I've been changed." What we all share in common is clarity about a "before" and an "after" being taken up into Christ's God-consciousness. Before, we lived in the collective life of sin, dissatisfied underneath it all, unaware of the possibility of God-consciousness. After, we live in the collective life in grace, growing in our sense of blessedness, growing in the steadiness of Christ's God-consciousness. Before, we can identify a process of God's preparatory grace drawing us toward regeneration, the transition to the life in grace. After, we are in the life-long process of sanctification, growing in grace and blessedness. So in preparatory grace, we experience a process moving us toward a transition that we call "regeneration." In sanctification, we experience a process in which everything that was initiated at that transition grows and strengthens (§110). Clearly, we want to understand that transition, which Schleiermacher calls "regeneration," in greater detail. Everything hangs on it.

Schleiermacher looks at regeneration, the transition, from two points of view: God's and our own (§107). What is happening in regeneration from God's point of view is called "justification." What is happening in regeneration from the human point of view is called "conversion." From both points of view, regeneration results in the establishment of a new kind of relationship between an individual and God. The character of that relationship is patterned on the relationship that Christ has with God and is growing toward the perfection of Christ's relationship with God. Justification and conversion are simultaneous.

From God's point of view—justification—two things establish the new relationship (§109): forgiveness for being closed to intimate relationship and adoption as a child of God. These two aspects represent the beginning of intimacy through being taken up with Christ. Schleiermacher does not engage in further speculation about what had to occur within God in order for God to forgive and welcome us as God's own. He describes what we experience God having done in establishing a new relationship. Forgiveness is the end of the old relationship, being closed to God, and being adopted as a child of God designates the beginning of the new one. They happen simultaneously; the old one ends as the new one begins.

God, through the original divine decree of redemption through Christ, made forgiveness and adoption available from the beginning of time. Justification, both forgiveness and adoption, is actualized only when we assent to begin the relationship with God through trusting faith in Christ. God does not establish intimate relationship with us without our being open to it. Thus, we experience justification only when our trust in Christ allows us to enter the relationship with God that God has been offering all along. In Schleiermacher's systematic language, we affirm that we are justified by faith. This concept is clarified further when we examine regeneration from the human point of view.

To sum up thus far, let us add to our diagram the terms we've discussed:

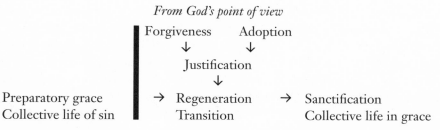

Schleiermacher uses the term "conversion" to designate everything involved from the human point of view in regeneration/the transition (§108). Just as for God, the old ends and the new begins. The ending, from the human point of view, is repentance. The beginning is faith. Each of these can be explored further. Repentance includes a feeling of regret about the past, about having been closed to intimacy with God. But in addition to regret, an actual change of heart occurs, a change to readiness to receive the gift of intimacy offered through Christ. Once intimacy is received, the old life is gone. Anytime reflections of it show up, we fight against them as soon as we recognize them. The choice to receive intimacy, our change of heart, is permanent; otherwise the transition isn't real, and we're still in the realm of preparatory grace.

What begins in conversion is faith. We appropriate Christ's God-consciousness, his perfectly open trust of God's guiding his awareness, which is to say that we trust God is empowering us to live in intimate relationship of the kind Christ has with God. Thus faith is living in trusting relationship. In Schleiermacher's use of the term, faith has nothing to do with ideas we believe; rather, faith is our way of living with God.

Again, we can summarize by adding these terms to our diagram:

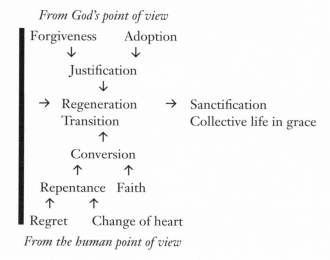

How might we characterize the underlying feeling that we experience at each stage of the process of redemption? Schleiermacher calls the feeling that underlies the collective life of sin "misery." Some of us might find the characterization "dissatisfaction" more accurate. Schleiermacher uses a word that doesn't translate very well, *Unlust*, meaning the absence of pleasure or desire. Without intimate relationship with God we feel in one way or another our incompleteness as human beings. In contrast to this, we experience the collective life in grace as one of growing blessedness. From regeneration forward through sanctification our underlying gratitude and joy increase. In some moments these feelings may be obscured by temporary events, but the presence of blessedness remains and increases. We anticipate the fulfillment that is unfolding in the world through divine love.

Each of the terms we have explored is used in a variety of very different ways in other theological systems. Describing all the different uses would take a book of its own. More importantly, comparing other ways of using the terms will not clarify at all what Schleiermacher has done. The entire diagram of relationships between terms must be considered together in order to see the experience that Schleiermacher is trying to illuminate. Focusing on one term apart from the others begins a quibble over words and allows us to avoid being challenged or invited to take in the magnitude of the experience of redemption being described.

> Pause for a moment to notice your feelings about redemption as it is laid out before you now.
>
> Have any aspects of your experience of redemption been left out of Schleiermacher's account?
>
> Where would you add them to his picture, or does the picture of redemption have to be entirely redesigned in order to include your experience?

SEVEN BIBLICAL STORIES

We can't think about Christ without interpreting seven major biblical stories about his life that are told or alluded to in the New Testament. These are the virgin birth (in Matthew and Luke), baptism (in Matthew, Mark, and Luke), miracles (all four Gospels), resurrection (all four Gospels), ascension (in Luke and Acts), return for last judgment (in Matthew and Mark), and preexistence as Word of God (John). By now, we can anticipate that Schleiermacher interprets at least some of the major pieces of the story of Christ in unfamiliar ways. Before we investigate how Schleiermacher interprets these accounts, let us first remind ourselves how he understands the role of Scripture in forming and guiding Christian faith.

Scripture cannot be the foundation for Christian faith; faith in Christ must exist before someone gives Scripture special authority (§128). At first, this statement may sound shocking, but the reasons behind it invite us to continue thinking clearly about our faith. Schleiermacher is consistent in his thinking. The experience of redemption is the ground of our faith. We experience redemption as the effect of the communication of Christ's sinless perfection, his unbroken God-consciousness. That experience of redemption is the same for us as it was for Christ's first followers. They received the experience through personal encounter, seeing in the words and the actions of Jesus what the fulfillment of human life is like. Then, as they received the God-consciousness of Christ into their own lives, they opened the way through themselves for the next generation to encounter that same God-consciousness of Christ, the same relationship to God. Faith passes from person to person and generation to generation, because God-consciousness is articulated and otherwise made visible in the lives of faithful people.

Notice that the first followers of Christ did not have Scripture on which to ground their faith. Neither did the next generation. They only had personal encounter with those who had been redeemed. Scripture is a text that helps guarantee that our witness to Christ today is the same as the original witness. But what grounds faith is the living witness to the experience of redemption, not the text. Scripture alone, without the church's witness to the living experience of redemption, would be lifeless.

We might ask Schleiermacher, why can't Christ speak directly to persons today? Why does his influence only come through other people? His answer is quite straightforward. If someone were to claim that a revelation came to them directly from Christ, that claim would have to be confirmed before others in the community of faith could accept it. The confirmation can only come by comparing the revelation to the faith that has been lived and passed on from generation to generation. Recall that Schleiermacher was a pastor. Early in his career he was chaplain to the hospital in Berlin that included caring for mentally ill persons. Schizophrenic persons often have personal and unique religious visions, including Christ interacting with them quite closely. In response to this kind of vision, Schleiermacher suggests that the faith of the Christian community is a faith that is visible and available to all persons and that it is available to all who will receive it rather than being limited to a select few who receive visions. Redemption, as Schleiermacher has interpreted it, requires physical individuals who are living in intimate relationship with God to communicate its reality. Direct visions from Christ cannot do this, and for this reason they are not part of the church's faith.

Thus, Scripture has a premier place in Christianity because it is the earliest written testimony of Christians to the influence of Christ. Scripture is the record of early faith through Christ, and for this reason we check our own testimony to Christ against it. But as a record of human faith, rather than a product of dictation from God, Scripture can and does include peripheral details and notions that can obscure the central reality of the redemption brought about by Christ (§129). The task of every thoughtful reader of Scripture is to critically discern what is central and to set to one side what is peripheral. The standard we use in this discernment is the community of faith's experience of redemption over the past two thousand years.

At this point it is especially important to understand the thoughts and feelings we have about our own faith's basic relationship to Scripture. Which of the following approaches is closest to your own thoughts and feelings? Are your feelings closer to one approach and your thinking closer to another?

1. Scripture is the source of faith; we encounter Christ directly through Scripture, and he speaks to us personally in Scripture.

2. Scripture historically and accurately shows us who Christ is, and we believe in response to what we see and are told about Christ.

3. Faith is validated by Scripture; we know that we have faith because our faith matches Scripture's picture of true faith in Christ.

4. We know we live in faith through Christ; Scripture confirms our expressions of our faith by providing patterns for how to express it.

Because he has interpreted the beginning point and touchstone for Christian faith as the experience of redemption through Christ, Schleiermacher is closest to the fourth approach.

Schleiermacher's touchstone for faith makes it easier for persons who share modern skepticism about supernatural events to be consistent in their faith and their thinking about the world. We can see Schleiermacher's approach in his interpretation of specific features of the biblical account of Christ. The resurrection is the feature most frequently associated with redemption in other theological interpretations; we see the nuances of Schleiermacher's interpretation if we start with Christ's resurrection and then turn to the beginning of his life and proceed through it.

The resurrection is not a part of the redeeming activity of Christ, in Schleiermacher's interpretation of redemption (§99). He has three reasons for this conclusion. First, the resurrection is not an activity of Christ himself, but instead is an act of God on Christ; "God raised him from the dead" is the biblical testimony. The God-consciousness that is manifest and perfected in Christ is not proved or influenced at all by the resurrection. The incarnation of this God-consciousness makes redemption possible. Second, the resurrection does not follow as a logical outcome following the death of the one who redeems in the way that Christ redeems. The resurrection is a surprise. Third, the first followers of Christ recognized him as the Son of God, a sure sign that they had experienced redemption, before Christ's death and resurrection. If resurrection is part of the redeeming activity of Christ, this recognition was not possible (§99.1). If resurrection is essential to redemption through Christ, then the Gospel testimony that the disciples recognized Jesus as the Son of God must have been a false memory, a projection back from the postresurrection experience. Schleiermacher prefers not to consider the recognition of Christ's relationship to God that is given in the Gospels as a false memory or projection.

This decision to be consistent in interpreting Scripture in light of the community of faith's experience of redemption from the beginning gives Christians today freedom in our thinking about Christ's resurrection. Belief in Christ's resurrection is not an essential component of redemption through Christ. If a Christian believes the Gospel accounts of resurrection, the reason for such belief is that the Christian has found an account convincing as a historical record of events. Belief in resurrection is a historical judgment based on the historical evidence, not a test of faith. Schleiermacher himself thinks good historical reason exists to believe the resurrection occurred. Strong, multiple testimony to it comes from the very witnesses whose testimony to the experience of redemption made it possible for the next generation to experience redemption, and that same person-to-person testimony is the means through which Christ influences us today. So if those first witnesses, who were reliable when it came to redemption, all agree that Christ was resurrected, Schleiermacher trusts their account. However, he accepts that some Christians, who have also experienced redemption through Christ, may come to a different evaluation of the evidence.

But what about the apostle Paul's emphasis on believing Christ was raised? Schleiermacher points to the entirety of Paul's argument in 1 Corinthians 15 as the expression of Paul's full thought on the matter, and he interprets everything Paul says in light of it (§99.1). In that argument, the resurrection of Christ is the guarantee of our own resurrection, but not, however, evidence of the divine indwelling in Christ. So in Schleiermacher's reading of Paul, Paul does not link redemption to the resurrection. On the other hand, Paul does speak of Christ as the second Adam, the perfection of human nature, which is consistent with Schleiermacher's account of redemption. So in Schleiermacher's reading of Paul, the resurrection functions for Paul as a way of expressing the absolute change that is possible for human beings as a result of Christ's incarnation.

We see a similar pattern of analysis and conclusions as we examine the other six stories.

Schleiermacher thinks through the account of the virgin birth of Christ from two different directions: from the point of view of the New Testament witness to it and from the point of view of whether the event helps explain Christ's sinless perfection. From both points of view, he concludes that belief in a virgin birth is not an essential part of faith in Christ as our redeemer (§97.2).

From the point of view of the New Testament witness, Schleiermacher emphasizes the following features: The stories in Matthew and Luke are never referred to again in the New Testament, not even in those Gospels. If the stories were essential to faith, surely they would have been at least alluded to again. The early religious texts that make much of Christ's birth were expressly excluded from the New Testament canon, another indication that the early church knew these stories to be peripheral. Schleiermacher also notes that the Gospel of John makes no effort to correct the impression made when Jesus is called the son of Joseph. The New Testament witness to the importance of believing that Jesus was born of a virgin is not strong.

From the point of view of explaining Christ's sinless perfection, the virgin birth is not at all useful. The fathering of Christ can only have importance if it either explains how Christ avoided original sin or explains how the new form of God-consciousness came to exist in a human being. A divine conception would not explain either one, according to Schleiermacher. As to original sin, an immaculate conception of every woman in Mary's ancestry all the way back to Eve would have been neccessary in order to avoid the effects of the sin of previous generations. Such a chain of virginal conceptions is ridiculous and nowhere claimed in Christian faith. As for the introduction of God-consciousness in human being, Schleiermacher *does* see this event as super-natural. Christ's God-consciousness could not have developed naturally out of human nature, but had to have been introduced from outside human nature, hence the name "super-natural." But in Schleiermacher's view, reproduction could not introduce something new into human being. We might disagree with him on that point because of our contemporary understanding of genetic mutation. But he might well respond to our point that genetics do not very adequately explain spiritual characteristics. So at the end of the dialogue with him on the point, he would still conclude that the virgin birth is inadequate by itself to explain Christ's sinless perfection.

In typical fashion for Schleiermacher, he concludes that acceptance of the virgin birth is not at variance with other aspects of Christian faith, so we can believe it if we want to. But because such belief is not essential to redemption, nor well testified in the New Testament, nor helpful in adequately explaining Christ's sinless perfection, requiring belief in the virgin birth by all Christians is not acceptable (§97.2). All that is required is that we recognize in Christ a new power that comes from outside human nature and that completes human nature.

The baptism of Jesus by John is narrated all the Gospels except John. Schleiermacher, however, minimizes its importance in order to be consistent in his idea that Christ's God-consciousness was perfect throughout his human life (§103.2). Christ's baptism is neither a transfer of authority nor a transition within Christ's own self-awareness, but simply an action marking the transition between Christ's private life and his public life. This transition is from the point of view of others, but not within Christ himself. By associating himself with John the Baptist, Christ gave people who had never encountered him a specific opinion about him. This opinion provided a place for Christ to begin his teaching about himself and the reign of God that was founded through faith in him.

The Gospels each narrate a number of miracles, and the question of how to interpret those miracles was actively debated among Protestant Christian scholars during Schleiermacher's lifetime. For the most part Schleiermacher sidestepped the question of whether a Christian had to believe that Christ performed acts that broke the known laws of nature. Miracles are superfluous for redemption through Christ; they don't help us to receive his God-consciousness (§103.1). The only miracle that matters is the appearance of Christ's sinless perfection in a living human person, which is not really a miracle. Instead, the appearance of the Redeemer is part of the unfolding of God's original creation—part of the intention for nature, though not an intention we could achieve on our own. As he did with the virgin birth, Schleiermacher considered miracles from two points of view: how they were described in Scripture, and how they might function in theological thinking (§103.1). Schleiermacher noted that in Scripture miracles were attributed to many persons, especially to prophets. Those miracles served to evoke trust in the prophets' short-term predictions, which helped convince people to do what needed to be done immediately. But Schleiermacher contrasts the role of the prophets with the role of Christ. Faith in Christ does not involve trusting predictions at all, and the spiritual power of Christ is evident in his entire life at every moment. So Christ never used a miracle to confirm a prediction, much less to evoke faith. Once in a while, a miracle might have led someone to recognize Christ for what he was, but the ground of the faith was Christ himself, not the miracle. Christ used his powers to do good, just as every person does. Since he was perfectly open to God his performing of miracles is possible. However, belief in the accounts of miracles is not part of redemption. The way in which we believe the New Testament accounts is a feature of our relationship to Scripture, not a part of our relationship to God through Christ.

We have already looked in detail in the previous chapter at how Schleiermacher interprets the suffering and death of Christ, and we began our discussion in this section with the resurrection. The next major event in the New Testament account of Christ is the ascension (§99). Just like the resurrection, belief in the ascension is not a necessary part of redemption. But Schleiermacher evaluates the sources for the account of the ascension with more skepticism than the resurrection accounts (§99.2). Ascension stories appear only in Luke and Acts, both written by the same author. Further, Schleiermacher determined on the basis of what Luke himself says that he was not an eyewitness to the events he narrated. Schleiermacher does not find the accounts of the ascension believable. Since the ascension is neither essential to the experience of redemption nor well-attested historically, Schleiermacher views it peripherally.

The next feature of the New Testament account of Christ is his return to judge the earth (§99). Schleiermacher takes special care to discuss the last judgment and other doctrines concerning last things (including the consummation of the church, bodily resurrection, and immortality of the soul) because they are common beliefs among Christians (§157–§162). Nevertheless, when belief in the last judgment is considered from his starting point— our experience of redemption through Christ—Schleiermacher concludes that this belief is peripheral, neither part of nor directly related to redemption. In other words, the God-consciousness we receive through Christ is not connected to a belief in life after death or belief in a final judgment.

As with the other stories of Christ, Schleiermacher considers final judgment from two directions, interpreting New Testament accounts and working systematically from redemption. In a number of places in the Gospels, Christ predicts a final judgment. Almost all of them are in Matthew. Schleiermacher concludes that a final judgment was Matthew's concern rather than Christ's concern. Unlike the resurrection, which was attested in all four Gospels, final judgment is not decisively expressed as part of Christ's message in all four. Schleiermacher does not delve into the exegesis that supports this conclusion in *Christian Faith*, but he does in his exegetical lectures. This topic is one of the places where his exegesis in 1830 differs significantly from exegesis of the Gospels today.

How does final judgment fit in with our central Christian faith experience and beliefs? Schleiermacher observes that Christian belief in a final judgment primarily expresses a vengeful desire to increase the misery of unbelievers, or it expresses a fear that Christians might have that if they are in the company of the "bad," they will experience more pain themselves (§162.3). Obviously neither of these perspectives expresses a perfected communion with Christ— whose communion with God was utterly untouched by the condition of the persons around him, and whose mission was to make plain the possibilities of intimate relationship with God and thus the possibility of an end to misery. Schleiermacher explores in detail different versions of Christian beliefs having to do with last things and repeatedly observes that the beliefs cannot be expressed in such a way that they are both consistent with each other and consistent with our experience of redemption. He is careful not to say that Christians should not believe in a last judgment, but the belief is clearly not necessary for true faith in Christ. The community of faith ought to watch that expressions of belief in last judgment are not simply expressions of vengefulness or fear of outsiders.

> This interpretation of last judgment as a peripheral belief is striking in its force. Notice how you feel about it.
>
> Now, engage in conversation with Schleiermacher. If you disagree with his analysis, what are the points you would emphasize to convince him to reconsider? If you agree with his analysis, what additional arguments would you make?

Discussion of the preexistence of Christ as the Word of God or as part of the Trinity does not belong in a system of doctrine, according to Schleiermacher. He offers two reasons for his claim. First, he determined at the very beginning of his account that only ideas that are derived from Christian consciousness are appropriately a part of Christian doctrine. Ideas unrelated directly to what Christians experience thus do not apply. Not even the first followers of Christ experienced his preexistence, nor can any Christian since. We can know Christ only once he "became flesh," which is to say as the fully human, fully divine person who lived among us. So the opening verses of the Gospel of John are speculative and an act of praise, but are not a source for a system of doctrine.

The second reason for avoiding discussing the preexistence of Christ is that through the course of Christian history all of the attempts at such discussion have led to significant difficulties. Usually these difficulties lead to an outright error, describing Christ in such a way that he could not be fully human (§105, postscript). In §94 and §95 of *Christian Faith*, Schleiermacher addresses these many difficulties each in turn and concludes that we cannot discuss the preexistence of Christ intelligibly and remain consistent with what we know from our own experience of him during his life. We return in the next section to the implications for the doctrine of the Trinity of this decision not to discuss the preexistence of Christ.

Consistent with this decision is Schleiermacher's conclusion that Christ could not have had any foreknowledge of his preexistence that he could share with his followers. A fully human person could not comprehend such knowledge of himself. The perfection of Christ was a perfection of the human God-consciousness, nothing more and nothing less. Attributions of other kinds of perfection to Christ are thus also unwarranted (§93.2). His appearance, his physical abilities, and his intelligence were all within the range of normal human ability. No need to claim that they were extraordinary exists because those features of being human have no direct bearing on God-consciousness. Christ is the perfection of human relationship with God. Nothing more needs to be claimed about him.

Christians often read portions of the Hebrew Bible to point toward or prefigure the coming of Christ into the world. Schleiermacher argues that such readings thoroughly misunderstand the uniqueness of Christ. His God-consciousness could not be anticipated until it appeared in human history. Consequently, none of the prophecies of a coming Messiah could possibly be pointing toward someone like Christ; he simply could not be imagined. Christ came among a people and at a time in human history when persons would be able to recognize and respond to his God-consciousness. Thus, that Christ was a Jew matters, but what he initiated is dramatically different from Judaism in Schleiermacher's view. This way of thinking points toward the uniqueness of Christian faith, protects the integrity of Jewish interpretations of their own sacred texts from Christian appropriation, and is also consistent with unfolding Christian doctrine only from the experience of Christ himself.

This place in the discussion is a good point to notice the effect of the way Schleiermacher has gone about his theological thinking. He has identified and carefully described the central component of Christian faith. Then in thinking about every other feature of Christianity, he shows how it relates to that central component, which makes his description of Christian faith consistent and systematic. But if a belief or practice of Christians does not relate to the central component of Christian faith, this way of thinking theologically leads to one of two conclusions. Either the belief or practice directly contradicts the central component—in which case it is false and should be excluded from the practices accepted in the community of faith—or the belief or practice is peripheral to Christian faith and Christians can agree to disagree about it. A peripheral belief or practice should never be used to exclude persons from the community of faith. In this approach to thinking theologically, the way in which the central component of Christianity is identified and described makes a big difference.

What advantages and disadvantages with this way of thinking systematically can you identify?

Some theologians disagree with Schleiermacher's systematic way of thinking theologically. Other theologians agree with thinking systematically but disagree with his definition of the central component of the Christian faith. Which of these two positions can you find more reasons to support?

A striking aspect of Schleiermacher's account is the diversity of Christian beliefs that are embraced within it. A redeemed Christian may believe in the resurrection and ascension of Christ as described in the New Testament and be in communion and community with a redeemed Christian who is unable to accept either account. Similarly a Christian may believe in the virgin birth and in miracles—or not. The *faith* of those who have experienced redemption through Christ brings together a community of faith with very different *beliefs* about what is not essential. The faith is essential. Schleiermacher's systematic interpretation of Christian faith does not include everyone, however. For example, people who disagree with him about what is essential to faith and what is peripheral belief are not included. In Schleiermacher's own time, he recognized that Roman Catholics would specify some peripheral beliefs in his account as essential in their own. He still recognized them as Christian, but they could not share one theology.

> Does setting yourself apart from Christians whose beliefs are different from your own make you uncomfortable, or is it an important way to be clear about your own beliefs?
> What kinds of activities do you think Christians can or should engage in together in spite of our theological differences?

At the end of this section, let us recall what we saw in the previous chapter about the many features of the Gospel stories that Schleiermacher took very seriously and on which he built his portrait of Christ and Christ's effectiveness. We have looked in this section at seven stories that are not central to Christian faith. Far more accounts, especially of Christ's teaching, are available with which Schleiermacher has painted his portrait of the Redeemer.

THE CHURCH'S DOCTRINE OF THE TRINITY AND THE HOLY SPIRIT

Up to this point in our exploration of Christology, we have limited our account to what we can say based upon human encounter with God in the world. We have examined what we can say concerning our life before and after experiencing redemption through Christ, and we have limited our statements about who Christ is and also about how he is related to God to what is evident to us as a direct result of the experience of redemption. Schleiermacher set up his entire account in this fashion from the very beginning; everything in Christianity is related to the redemption Christ has wrought. Schleiermacher refrains from saying anything that is not evident as a result of Christian experience of redemption. As a result, he leaves to the end of his systematic account any discussion of the Trinity.

The difficulty with the traditional versions of the doctrine of the Trinity (Father, Son, and Holy Spirit) is that the doctrine is speculative. We do not have direct experience that leads us to posit the three persons of the Trinity as separate individuals. The New Testament witness to the individual three persons is ambiguous, and the doctrine of each of the three existing equal to the one supreme divine being and the one supreme divine being existing equal to each of the three is not found in the New Testament at all. The doctrine of the Trinity is like the resurrection and the ascension in that we may believe it if we choose, but it is not a direct part of our experience of faith. Furthermore, even though Christian creeds declare that formula is true, the various attempts through Christian history to explain how it is true all end up falling into the error of one of the earliest theologians, Origen. He declared that the Father is unqualifiedly God, but the Son and the Holy Spirit are God only through their participation in the divine nature. Obviously then, they are not equal with the Father. Even as a speculative doctrine, the Trinity has not been explained in a consistent way (§170.1; §170, postscript; §171; §171.1).

So where does Schleiermacher take us in his account of God? On the basis of our experience of God in the world as a result of our redemption through Christ, he provides the following account. We experience one attribute of God directly in redemption: God is love. Divine love is seen in redemption as the divine essence communicating itself in and through the world. The only other attribute of God that we experience directly is a perfection of love; that attribute is wisdom. The world and time itself were created in such a way that, through time and the world, the almighty love of God is presented more and more perfectly, which offers evidence of the wisdom of God. Formally this concept can be expressed as follows: "Divine wisdom is the principle that orders and determines the world for the divine self-impartation that is carried out in redemption" (§168). The purpose of creation itself appears to us as a result of our experience of redemption simply to unfold as the object of divine love (§169.2).

In addition to these two attributes of God, two other points are clear to us as a result of our experience of redemption. First, the being of God is in Christ. We can say this confidently in light of all of our earlier accounts of redemption and of Christ. The New Testament use of the title "Son of God" points to this attribute, but we move beyond our experience of redemption if we try to make the title mean more than that the being of God is in Christ. The whole account that we examined in chapter 5 is intended to explain how we can understand what that single phrase means. No more can be said here unless we move into speculation beyond our human experience and ability to know.

The second item that is clear from our Christian self-consciousness after redemption is that the being of God is in the Christian church, although not in every individual equally (§117). We recognized this concept earlier in the description of regeneration. Inner and outer circles of the Christian community exist. The "elect" are those who live in the community of redemption; they participate in the blessedness of Christ—that is, they are regenerate. The "called" are those on whom preparatory grace is at work through the influence of the regenerate, drawing the "called" toward redemption and blessedness (§117.1).

The being of God works in the church through its influence on the regenerate. In other words, the life of Christ is in us as a common spirit. A third way to say the same thing is that the Holy Spirit is leading us as a community of faith (§124.1, §124.2). Any one of those ways of speaking is acceptable in the church. However, we clearly cannot do without Christ or go beyond Christ, nor can we do without the community of faith. After Christ physically left the earth following his resurrection, the effectiveness of Christ came to be and is manifest through the community of faith, the church. The effectiveness of Christ is the being of God in him, so his effectiveness in the church must be the being of God in it as the common Spirit of Christ. The Spirit of Christ and the Holy Spirit are two ways of referring to the same reality in the church (§121.2). Thus, being taken up into the life of Christ and participating in the Holy Spirit are the same thing.

Thinking about the Holy Spirit in this way, as the being of God in the church, requires us to let go of the most common way we think of the Holy Spirit—as if it were a person with separate being and activity. Schleiermacher suggests that "Holy Spirit" is simply the name we give to the being of God present in and influencing the community of faith. In the same way, Christ is the name we give to the being of God in a human being who is perfectly open to the being of God and whose person is completely formed by the presence of the being of God in him. If we think about it this way, we stretch our minds a bit, but we avoid most of the difficulties involved in a doctrine of the Trinity. We instead refer to one being of God by different names under different circumstances.

After the ascension of Christ, the being of God that perfected human nature in him and effected redemption in his first followers was present in the community of those first followers. The being of God drew that community into a unity with one another that was striking to all who encountered the community—"see how they love one another!" The community as a whole became the image of Christ in the world. Individuals can never be adequate images of Christ because we will always bear the influence of our former experience in the collective life of sin, if not through some old habits, at least through the way our past shaped our personalities (§125.1). Only the community of faith, if we leave aside the influence of our former sin, can reflect all of the different features of the image of Christ's perfection; each of us reflects a portion of the image of Christ and only together do we reflect the fullness of the being of God in Christ. Only if we look at the church in this way can we see its purity; otherwise the influence of the collective life of sin obscures the true nature of the community of faith and what it is becoming, however slowly.

We began our theological reflection by thinking about Christ, but Christ is related to all of the concepts we use to account for our faith. The way we think about Christ influences how we think about the Trinity and about our experience of the Holy Spirit in the church. Schleiermacher has chosen to be systematic and consistent in his account of Christ and his account of the Holy Spirit, and this approach leads him to set aside the doctrine of the Trinity in its traditional forms in order to account for our actual experience of the being of God in the world, in Christ, and in the church. His account is Trinitarian in form and faithful to what we can say based on our experience of redemption and the earliest testimony of the followers of Christ.

> Schleiermacher's entire account is limited to what can be said about God based upon the human experience of redemption through Christ. What advantages do you see to limiting a theological account in this way so that it excludes speculation about God? What disadvantages do you see to limiting a theological account in this way? The discussion of the Trinity may give you some examples of both advantages and disadvantages.
>
> Do you yourself prefer theological accounts that limit themselves to human experience of God, or do you prefer theological accounts that engage in some speculation about the being of God beyond human experience of God in the world?

The forceful claim that Schleiermacher makes is that after the ascension of Christ, the church alone is the bearer and perpetuator of the redemption brought about through Christ. Christians don't end up participating in a church simply because some of us are social and want to be part of a group, while others who are more introverted are just fine living outside of a community of faith. Schleiermacher claims that we can only experience redemption in the context of a community of faith, because the Holy Spirit works through the regenerate in the community to evoke in others the experience of being taken up into the God-consciousness of Christ that is redemption. So we start out in the community of faith, we experience redemption there, and we stay because that is where the being of God is at work—where the Holy Spirit is active in us and the community as a whole through us.

Obviously Schleiermacher's account at this juncture is an account from the point of view of Christians who are part of a community of faith. His perspective not only expresses the point of view of persons within a community of faith, it implies that people who call themselves "Christian" but who choose not to participate in a community of faith cannot have experienced redemption and blessedness through Christ. Schleiermacher does not specify that a community of faith must be a part of an institutional church, but his silence on the matter suggests his assumption that communities of faith are found within institutional churches.

The way Schleiermacher began his account of Christian faith as an experience of Christians in the church led him pretty directly to the conclusion just named, but a lot of the content of his account is connected directly or indirectly to this point. How might a Christian who is not part of a community of faith respond to Schleiermacher's account?

How could his account be adapted to recognize Christian faith existing outside the context of a community of faith? Do you find this adapted account to be equally compelling?

7

An Evaluative Look at the Picture

Forming One's Own View

We have only two tasks left in our thinking about Christ with Schleiermacher. We must bring together all of the pieces we have begun to articulate concerning our own thinking about Christ, and we must evaluate the strengths and the deficiencies of Schleiermacher's thinking about Christ and of our own.

RETURN TO AN OVERALL VIEW

Six questions enable us to bring the overall picture of Christ into focus. These questions come from within a Christian point of view. They assume that Christ is a central figure in our religious experience. We are exploring a conceptual picture of Christ designed to interpret and thereby support Christian religious experience.

How are we different as a result of redemption, and what is our Christian hope? Schleiermacher's answer is that we have left the collective life that is out of relationship with God and we have entered the collective life in grace, in which our relationship with God is growing toward perfection. We experience through Christ the possibility of sensing God's presence in our immediate awareness in every moment and translating that sense into every thought, emotion, and action that we have. This experience yields a growing blessedness, an unshakeable joy. Our hope is that the intimacy with God and the joy that we experience now is a foretaste of the perfection of both.

What did Christ do (or what does Christ do) to bring about this result? Christ was the fulfillment of human being in relationship with God. His entire life made visible the intimacy and joy that are God's intention for human life. What Christ did was to make his inner life in relationship with God visible through his preaching and his actions. His unique *Urbildlichkeit* draws us to him and conveys the power to live in the same intimate relationship with God.

Which features of human life are involved in this account? Schleiermacher describes an immediate awareness that occurs in the moment between when something stirs us (from without or within) and when we translate that stirring into a thought, emotion, or action. Schleiermacher assumes a normal pattern of development in human thinking abilities, emotional maturity, and physical skills. He also recognizes that humans flourish in community and that faith is communicated in and supported by community.

Which features of God are involved in this account? The single divine decree in which God generates the whole unfolding of creation in love. God's continued participation through love is seen both in God's presence in Christ and in God's presence in the community of faith.

What must be true about Christ for him to have the redemptive effect that he has? In every moment of his entire life Christ was completely open to the presence of God in his immediate awareness, and he translated this openness into every thought and act. It is the being of God in him. He made this sinless perfection, this God-consciousness, visible to people who spent any time with him.

How is this account of Christ substantiated and warranted? Schleiermacher substantiates his account by referring at each point both to the New Testament narrative and to Christian experience of living in faith. He interprets these references in light of ordinary standards of reasonableness. The only warrant for faith he acknowledges is the actual experience of living in relationship with God through Christ.

Take the time you need now to answer each of these questions about your own account of Christ.

1. How are we different as a result of redemption, and what is our Christian hope?
2. What did Christ do (or what does Christ do) to bring about this result?
3. Which features of human life are involved in this account?
4. What features of God are involved in this account?
5. What must be true about Christ for him to have the redemptive effect that he has?
6. How is this account of Christ substantiated and warranted?

WITHIN THE LIMITS OF THE CHALCEDONIAN DEFINITION OF ORTHODOXY?

We are now at a point where we can evaluate the account Schleiermacher has provided and the accounts of Christ we have begun to develop. In the history of Christianity, the definition of faith in Christ that was hammered out by the ecumenical council held in 451 C.E. in Chalcedon is the standard for orthodoxy. As we noted earlier, this definition does not explain how to think about Christ, but simply sets the boundaries for thinking.

Two things must both be true of Christ in an orthodox account. First, Christ must be perfect in Godhead *and* must be perfect in his humanity. In other words, Christ must be truly God and truly human—like us in all things except for sin. But second, Christ must have both of those natures without confusion, without change, without division, and without separation. He is not a split personality, not partly human and partly divine so that we can attribute some actions to his divinity and some actions to his humanity. Christ is one.

Explaining this concept is not easy, as we have seen. Four common errors slide outside those boundaries. Schleiermacher explicitly tries to avoid all four. In the first edition of *Christian Faith*, he labels these errors with traditional names that relate each to a theological perspective that lay outside the Chalcedonian definition of orthodoxy.[1]

The Manichean error is to understand human nature to be unredeemable or not perfectable. If this error were true, Christ could not have been fully human. Further, if one were still to argue for some form of redemption, it would have to separate us from our bodies and selves as we know them.

The Pelagian error is the opposite, understanding human nature to be within human control. Therefore, with sufficient effort or will on our part, we are certain to experience the results of redemption. Christ is thus not needed for redemption and is not even unique in his role as exemplar; others may also be examples to us in our effort to perfect ourselves. This approach naively ignores our common experience of being caught in sin and denies the social matrix that is given to us at birth, and which we can only marginally alter.

The Docetic error is to describe Christ in such a way that he appears human, but he is not really completely human. This error is easy to fall into while one is discussing the divine aspect of Christ. Schleiermacher agrees with the orthodox understanding that if Christ were not human in every aspect of his life, he could not redeem every aspect of our lives.

The Nazoretic error is to describe Christ so that he is only human and no different from the rest of us. The common view that Jesus was a great teacher or prophet or moral exemplar falls into this error. In this view, Christ has no power to free us from sin; all he can do is enlighten us in some fashion.

Schleiermacher's account of Christ, at least as we have described it, does in fact avoid each of these four errors. He avoids using the Greek concepts that the definition uses to distinguish between the "two natures" and the "person" of Christ. But he avoids these concepts in order to explain both the unity of Christ as one being and the perfect presence of the divine in a fully human being.

> Recognizing any of these four errors in our own account is not easy. After you look with a critical eye at your account for yourself, you might ask someone else to look at your account and see whether they recognize any of these four tendencies.

CONSISTENT WITH THE DOCTRINE OF THE TRINITY?

We have followed Schleiermacher's lead and have considered accounts of Christ entirely separately from the doctrine of the Trinity, of which Christ is one part. As we saw, Schleiermacher argued that the doctrine of the Trinity has significant difficulties as it has been articulated in the historic creeds of the ecumenical councils. One of the major problems is that the doctrine requires us to speculate about the being of God beyond our experience of God. But in spite of the difficulties, thinking through an account of Christ is not possible without relating that account to the doctrine of the Trinity at some point.

Schleiermacher's approach was to articulate the difficulties involved in the doctrine of the Trinity and then to show that the account of Christ which he provided was consistent with our threefold experience of God in the world. He then called for a rethinking of the doctrine of the Trinity, going back to the earliest articulations of faith recorded in the canon of the New Testament and considering them in light of Christian experience of faith through Christ. Schleiermacher died without attempting to produce such a full reexamination of the doctrine of the Trinity himself, and nothing quite like what he had in mind has been produced since. Later theologians have evaluated his reponse both positively and negatively. Rather than attempt to adjudicate that debate, we can find it more fruitful simply to think through the question for ourselves.

> You might find it helpful to review the last section of chapter 6 as you think through this question: Is your account of Christ consistent with the doctrine of the Trinity?
> How important is it that your account of Christ be consistent with the doctrine of the Trinity?

CONSISTENT WITH THE HISTORIC EXPERIENCE
OF FAITHFUL CHRISTIANS?

The next consideration as we evaluate a theological account is its consistency with the experience of faith both that contemporary Christians have and that Christians through the centuries have had. We noticed in chapter 3 that Christians with different growing edges describe redemption differently, and we acknowledged that one account of redemption could not adequately encompass all of those descriptions. First we find it helpful to note for persons on which growing edges this particular account is most helpful. *Christian Faith* is an account that works for persons whose growing edge is union with God. That book's approach is less comprehensible to persons whose growing edges involve self-mastery. Persons whose growing edges involve creating meaning and purpose can use the book to stretch our perception of faith beyond the things we do to who we are.

Having identified which Christians an account appeals to, the question remains of whether the account is useful. Does it invite Christians to grow further in faith, or does it give permission for us to be satisfied with the status quo? Does an account leave us with guilt that saps our energy for changing our lives in concrete ways? Does it strengthen our hope? Does an account help us to embrace the diversity within expressions of Christian faith while still defining clear boundaries for what is essential to that faith? Does it encourage Christians to think in an integrated way about all aspects of their lives? Schleiermacher's diverse congregation found his account as it came to expression in his preaching to be useful. One goal of this book has been to make his account clear enough to be useful to Christians in the twenty-first century as well.

Consider again your own account, however provisional it may seem to you. What sorts of people are most likely to find it appealing? Which growing edges does it address?

In what ways is your account useful to Christians? Look at the questions in the previous paragraph to help you answer this question.

DOES IT MAKE SENSE?

This question has two parts also. Is an account of Christ internally consistent, and is it externally consistent? Internal consistency is a question of whether the various ideas share the same assumptions and modes of expression. For instance, does a term refer to the same thing every time the term is used, whether referring to something in the divine realm or something in the human realm? Schleiermacher argues that the doctrine of the Trinity usually fails at this point of maintaining consistent reference for terms. His own account is very consistent, and on the basis of that consistency he boldly determined to leave out pieces of the story of Jesus that are very familiar.

External consistency means that an account does not contradict the best knowledge of the natural world and of human behavior that we have available in our culture. Sometimes Christian theologians will redefine the contents of the knowledge available from the culture in order to diminish contradictions with their account of Christ. Such redefinition compromises external consistency. The reason for striving for external consistency is to prevent Christians from having to divide their thinking into two categories: thinking when at work/school/fixing the car and thinking when faith is the topic. Schleiermacher strove for an account in which faith is related to every single thought, emotion, and action regardless of where we are or what we're doing. He took advantage of new ideas about human development to think both about redemption and about Christ himself. Similarly he took advantage of what are now studies in communication and in sociology to explain the role of the community of faith in effecting redemption. Because those fields have grown since their inception in Schleiermacher's time, aspects of his account are less nuanced than they would be if he were writing today. As knowledge in our culture changes, each generation has the challenge of developing a new or a more refined account of Christ.

> At this point, another reader can help us. Spotting inconsistencies is much easier in an account that is new to a reader than in an account that is very familiar. Where are there inconsistencies in your account of Christ?

DOES THE ACCOUNT FACILITATE ETHICAL ACTION?

The desire exists to be able to use theology, including an account of Christ, to stop Christians from being unduly influenced by the collective life of sin that was ours and in the midst of which we still live. To function in this way, theology needs a stronger imperative voice than Schleiermacher provides. Theologians tend to turn to some form of revelation from God to provide such a ground. Karl Barth provided an orthodox version of this tendency as he faced National Socialism in the 1930s. For Barth, revelation is neither directly given to an individual (which would require confirmation of the source from outside the revelation) nor simply found in the written words of Scripture (which include conflicting statements and therefore require analysis). Instead, revelation is given in the form of the Word behind the words including the Word behind the words in Scripture, in preaching, and in the historic affirmations of the church. In this way Barth allows for historical-critical readings of Scripture and yet retains the force of direct revelation. But only through faith does one know that the Word has been correctly identified. This point returns us to Schleiermacher's point of departure, the experience of the Christian community of faith. But Barth hides that point of departure behind a screen of certainty for the sake of making an imperative statement.

Latin American liberation theologians also use imperative statements, primarily concerning what they attribute to God—that is, a preferential option for the poor. This kind of imperative quickly clarifies the direction ethical action should take, thus weaving moral injunction into the account of faith itself.

Schleiermacher closely ties his account of doctrine, contained in *Christian Faith*, to his account of the life of action in the world that develops from faith through Christ. But he keeps these accounts distinct because each is a large undertaking in itself. He did not live long enough to publish the system of Christian ethics that he worked out in the six lecture courses he taught on the subject. The notes from his students that were published after his death reveal a system of Christian ethics as comprehensive and as complex as his account of Christian doctrine. Is it sufficient for the times in which we live to think through the task in two stages: the nature of Christian faith in Christ and then the implications of that faith for living as a Christian in a social, economic, political, cultural, and environmental context? Schleiermacher cannot answer that question for us, but we must ask it ourselves until we arrive at a clear answer.

> Think about how you and your community of faith use theological ideas. If Christian doctrine and Christian ethics are thought through sequentially, will you arrive at the point of thinking about Christian ethics, or will you bog down in the effort to clarify the fine points of theology? On the other hand, how will you proceed to think about Christian ethics if you are not initially clear about what constitutes the core of Christian faith through Christ? How will your ethics be specifically Christian? Are there times when Christianity must speak with an imperative voice? Could your current political or social or environmental circumstances be one of those times? How will you and your faith community know whether it is one of those times and what to say if it is?

WHAT BRIDGES ARE BUILT TO OTHER COMMUNITIES?

The questions and issues to think through in evaluation of a theological account don't get any easier as we proceed. A tension has been present within

Christianity since the very first ecumenical council in the fourth century. On the one hand, a theological account should be clear about what constitutes Christian faith and what is outside the experience of the community of faith. On the other hand, diversity exists within Christianity itself—in experience, in practice, and in expression of faith through Christ. So while a theological account should be clear about boundaries of the faith, such an account should also be capable of building bridges, at least to other theological accounts of Christian faith.

Schleiermacher's *Christian Faith* does very well at acknowledging a variety of theological accounts of redemption and accounts of Christ based on those accounts of redemption. We have seen where he names the basic criteria that all accounts must meet in order to be considered Christian. These criteria leave room for accounts that are more familiar in their reliance on traditional church language.

A second kind of bridge has become important to consider in the twenty-first century. The great historic faith traditions of the world are no longer practiced in isolation from one another. Christians and Jews and Moslems and Buddhists and Hindus live together in local communities and in a global economy and environment. To many people of faith, fostering accounts of one's own faith that help one to live comfortably with the significant differ-ences among the expressions of faith in these historic traditions seems to have gained in importance. So, we may choose to ask, how does a Christian theo-logical account of Christ help us to live with our neighbors who are not Christian?

Schleiermacher is of only limited help on this point. His description of the development of faith traditions in the introductory propositions of *Christian Faith* shows that in his account Christianity is the culmination of human reli-gious consciousness. No other faith has come as far, and no faith can surpass it. His confidence that the world is moving toward completion gives him simultaneous confidence that ultimately all human beings will experience redemption through Christ. This outlook is obviously triumphalist. On the other hand, this account also asserts that this result will occur in God's good time. We can do little to speed it up; redeeming all of humanity will take time. Further, in this understanding of redemption, forcing conversion on others is not possible. They will either see the God-consciousness of Christ guiding the actions of Christians, or they won't. If they don't, it is never entirely clear whether they aren't looking or the old habits from before redemption are obscuring what is growing in the inner life of the Christians with whom non-Christians come in contact.

How well does your account of Christ leave room for the possibility that other accounts within Christianity are true to the faith we share?

Do you think that it is important for Christians to talk about their own faith in ways that accept the value of other historic faith traditions? Why or why not?

If you think it is important, how does your account of Christ acknowledge the value of other historic faith traditions?

DOES THIS METHOD RECOMMEND ITSELF?

The final question we should ask ourselves does not concern the actual ideas we have in our account of Christ, but rather the way we approached creating the account itself. Does the starting point that we used for thinking about Christ recommend itself as a fruitful way to begin and organize our thinking? Could we have progressed further or avoided difficulties if we had begun at a different point?

The question with which Schleiermacher began was: What have we experienced as a result of our redemption through Christ? Joining him at this beginning point helped us avoid many of the difficulties involved in biblical scholarship that searches for the historical Jesus. Schleiermacher's starting point allowed us to think about something that we're confident every Christian has experienced, and discouraged us from trying to think speculatively about aspects of Christ to which we don't have access at all as historians (such as his preexistence as the Word). From this beginning question, we were led to consider not only the person and work of Christ, but also the nature of sin, the nature of God as we experience it in the world, and the Holy Spirit in the community of faith. From that one question, we could have explored connections to all the current doctrines of the church. (We didn't actually follow all of them, but Schleiermacher did.)

You may well have discovered that you have used a different starting place for thinking about Christ. If so, where does your starting place lead your thought? Does it avoid all the difficulties that Schleiermacher avoided? Does it avoid some places where you think Schleiermacher's account has difficulties?

Are there other aspects of Christian faith that you think might be explored by asking first about features of the common Christian experience of that aspect of faith?

As a careful reader, you have surely met the two main goals of this book at this point. You have explored the account of Christ that Schleiermacher provided, and you have practiced thinking theologically for yourself. Those are significant accomplishments; congratulations! You certainly know enough now not to expect that all the answers you seek can be found within this or any other book. They are found, if at all, as we live in openness to God and think carefully about what we experience in that relationship. Whether or not Schleiermacher's thought has brought you clarity, may the skills you have developed while you have thought alongside him serve you well.

Notes

Preface

1. Jane Vella, *Taking Learning to Task: Creative Strategies for Teaching Adults* (San Francisco: Jossey-Bass, 2000).
2. Richard R. Niebuhr, *Schleiermacher on Christ and Religion: A New Introduction* (New York: Charles Scribner's Sons, 1964).

Chapter 1

1. Wilhelm Dilthey, ed., *Aus Schleiermachers Leben*. In *Briefen*, 4 vols (Berlin: Georg Reimer, 1863), 4.176. The letter containing this statement is from Schleiermacher to a former student from Halle in 1810. Throughout this book, if an English source is not named, the translation is mine.
2. Friedrich Schleiermacher, *Der christliche Glaube nach den Grudsätzen der evangelischen Kirche in Zusammenhange dargestellt*, Band 1 und Band 2 (Berlin: Georg Reimer, 1821, 1822).
3. Friedrich Schleiermacher, *Der christliche Glaube nach den Grundsätzen der evangelischen Kirche im Zusammenhange dargestellt*, zweite Auflage, Band 1 und Band 2 (Berlin: Georg Reimer, 1830).
4. Friedrich Schleiermacher, *The Christian Faith: English Translation of the Second German Edition*, ed. H. R. Mackintosh and J. S. Stewart (Philadelphia: Fortress Press, 1928).
5. Friedrich Schleiermacher, *Sendschreiben über seine Glaubenslehre an Lücke*, ed. Hermann Mulert (Giessen: Alfred Töpelmann, 1908); English translation: *On the Glaubenslehre: Two Letters to Dr. Lücke*, trans. James Duke and Francis Fiorenza (Chico, Calif.: Scholars Press, 1981).
6. These concerns are, incidentally, the first theological concerns of any pastor who is responsible for the care of souls.
7. John H. Leith, ed., *Creeds of the Churches: A Reader in Christian Doctrine from the Bible to the Present*, rev. ed. (Atlanta: John Knox Press, 1973), 35–36.
8. Friedrich Schleiermacher, *Brief Outline of Theology as a Field of Study*, *Translation*

of the 1811 and 1830 editions, With Essays and Notes, trans. Terrence N. Tice (Lewiston, N.Y.: Edwin Mellen Press, 1990).

Chapter 2

1. Friedrich Schleiermacher, *On Religion: Speeches to its Cultured Despisers,* ed. Richard Crouter (Cambridge: Cambridge University Press, 1988).
2. Friedrich Schleiermacher, *Brief Outline of Theology as a Field of Study, Translation of the 1811 and 1830 editions, With Essays and Notes,* trans. Terrence N. Tice (Lewiston, N.Y.: Edwin Mellen Press, 1990). This work is also organized by propositions, and further footnotes will indicate the proposition number.
3. Schleiermacher, *Brief Outline,* §104.
4. German has two words that are both translated into English as the word "ethics." This fact presents a problem for us because Schleiermacher had very different and very specific meanings for each German term. *Ethik* involves the principles by which humans act as historical beings and is the study of human change and growth. *Sittenlehre* are the principles for how persons should act in light of their faith. Each system of doctrine implies its own set of such principles, because each interprets the faith in a particular way. I have used the English word "morals" to translate *Sittenlehre,* even though the English implies moralizing, which is not what Schleiermacher had in mind at all.
5. Schleiermacher, *Brief Outline,* §193.
6. Ibid., §198.
7. Ibid., §§213, 214.
8. Ibid., §330.
9. Ibid., §196.
10. Ibid., §203.
11. Ibid., §205.

Chapter 3

1. Immanuel Kant, *The Critique of Pure Reason,* trans. J. M. D. Meiklejohn (Chicago: Encyclopedia Britannica, 1952).
2. Immanuel Kant, *Religion within the Limits of Reason Alone,* trans. Theodore M. Greene and Hoyt H. Hudson (New York: Harper, 1960).

Chapter 4

1. See Gerald May, *Will and Spirit: A Contemplative Psychology* (San Francisco: Harper & Row, 1982), for a thorough account of the psychological dimensions of our resistance to intimacy with God. According to May, this struggle is a basic feature of deeper spirituality. His account offers encouragement for engaging in the struggle with great patience toward oneself and others.

Chapter 5

1. John H. Leith, ed., *Creeds of the Churches: A Reader in Christian Doctrine from the Bible to the Present,* rev. ed. (Atlanta: John Knox Press, 1973), 34–36.
2. Friedrich Schleiermacher, *The Life of Jesus,* ed. Jack C. Verheyden, trans. S. Maclean Gilmour (Mifflintown, Penn.: Sigler Press, 1997), 423–24.
3. Strauss, David Friedrich, *The Life of Jesus Critically Examined,* 4th ed., trans. George Eliot, ed. Peter Hodgson (1840; trans. 1892; reprint, Philadelphia: Fortress Press, 1972).

4. Schleiermacher, *Life of Jesus*, 15.
5. Ibid., 99.

Chapter 7

1. Schleiermacher, *Der christliche Glaube*, 1821 ed., vol. 1, §25, 93–96.

Index